A Lost Childhood

A Retrospective

By Lynda Williams

A LOST CHILDHOOD
A RETROSPECTIVE

ISBN 978-0-578-30596-7
Lynda Smith Williams LLC

www.lyndawilliamsauthor.com

Manufactured in the United States of America
First printing October 2021

Dedication to My Mother

This book is dedicated to my precious Mother, Mary B. Tison

She taught me to have faith in God. She knew only too well; it was the only "real" strength she had and taught me to live by faith and believe the Word of God. Life did not deal her a particularly good hand, but her faith in God remained strong.

In my opinion, she got the worst of all her marriage vows. However, she died still feeling lucky that R.C. Tison chose her for his wife. Not only was he a poor provider and husband, but he led her sons into a life of crime .... The one thing I don't think she ever forgave him for. I never understood her love and devotion to him considering what he put her through, but she asked me years ago not to questions it, just accept it, which I did.

She never, ever condoned any of my father or brothers' actions, rather she kept them in constant prayers and asked God to give them guidance and direction. My Mother was what is known as a "Prayer Warrior," she never ceased praying, even while going about daily chores.

My Mother remains in my heart forever...

I am not what happened to me...
I am what I choose to become

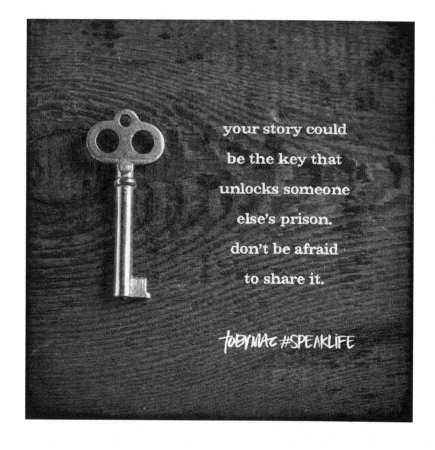

your story could
be the key that
unlocks someone
else's prison.
don't be afraid
to share it.

TOBYMAC #SPEAKLIFE

Contents

Preface

So many, many negative, critical thoughts and lies about myself and my circumstances growing up that always seemed stuck in my mind. I learned to silence them and voices saying that I could never be more than I was due to being a Tison, living on the south side of the tracks, and most probably being consider by many as white trash. This was based mostly on the criminal activities of my father and brothers always being in the news or on the front pages of newspapers. Most of my young life was spent feeling as though I was in the deep end of a swimming pool, with a leg cramp and nobody to help me. I learned to speak to those lies and negativity about who and what I was, and to fill my mind instead with what is good and beautiful about me, and not my unfortunate circumstances of growing up with career criminals and extreme abuse on every level.

My story is of the horrific lifestyle of being unfortunate enough to have been born into such a family, to include physical, emotional, and sexual abuse that I encountered within our home, generally daily. I learned the true meaning of "Fight or Flight" at an early age. As I wrote this book, I sometimes feel as though I'm projecting myself as being a saint, not having done anything wrong. The truth is, I made numerous mistakes throughout my life, mistakes I wish I could change, but I can't. However, in my heart I knew right from wrong and knew the environment of criminal activity and abuse that I was living in was abnormal, even at a young age. I had perfectly good examples my entire life

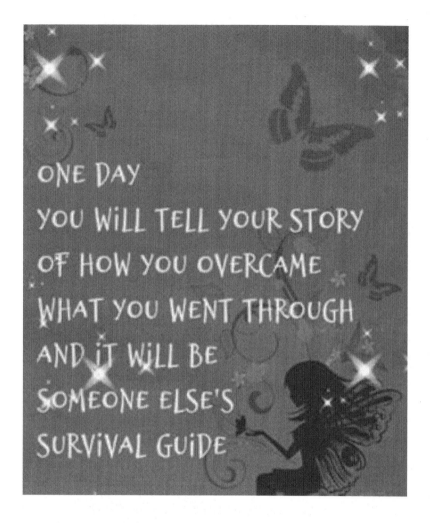

ONE DAY
YOU WILL TELL YOUR STORY
OF HOW YOU OVERCAME
WHAT YOU WENT THROUGH
AND IT WILL BE
SOMEONE ELSE'S
SURVIVAL GUIDE

growing up on *What Not to Do*. I knew there was a way out, and I fought to get there.

Writing about such an abusive upbring was not an easy thing to do, the memories came flooding back as I wrote. The highs and lows that sometimes looked promising, however, hurt so deeply. Fear was a daily part of my life as a young girl, the fear of physical as well as emotional abuse, right down to the fight for the last biscuit at breakfast. For the sake of survival, I learned to fight long before I learned to read and write.

Shame, which is something I experienced often growing up in such a dysfunctional family, and shame, as I learned from working in the mental health field, can be one of the most destructive of our human emotions. To heal from shame, was something I had to overcome, and was important for me to understand that *it was not my fault.*

I'm thankful for the gift of love and determina-tion that survived in my heart and my desire for the truth. I regret not one detail of my past, as incredibly embarrassing and painful as it was, my past has brought me to the person I have become, miraculously. I live in gratitude for the life I now have.

God's plan for me from the beginning was beyond my wildest dreams and imagination. I just knew in my heart, even as a young girl, there was a way out of the south side of the tracks and the dirty, disgusting lifestyle I had growing up with my father, RC, and my three brothers. My brothers took the same path as our father, for a life of crime, with RC as their mentor. I'm eternally grateful for the love of a Christian mother who tried to protect me as much as she possibly could and guide me toward a different path.

Working in the mental health field as an adult, we now understand the cycle of abuse. Unfortunately, fifty years ago we didn't. As a young woman, I found myself attracted to exactly what I thought I never wanted to be around again, not understanding my own behaviors and beliefs or the *Cycle of Abuse*. I ultimately married a man at a young age, exactly like my father, RC. He was emotionally as well as physically abusive, a womanizer and all those other labels that one can classify under the heading of a "bad husband." I tolerated it for years and thought if I were a good wife, mother, housekeeper, cook, and kept myself up, etc., he would change. However, it was just like growing up, thinking if I worked hard in the fields, helped mother in the house, made good grades in school, etc., RC would be nicer to me, however it never worked out that way. Working in the mental health field for so many years, I learned to understand we can't change others, only ourselves. My first husband, like RC, was incapable of change, as he too had lived a cycle of abuse in his own home growing up. Years ago, we knew nothing about correcting it except the empty promises they will never do it again, which were frequent.

Our last military duty station, with my then husband, was Key West, Florida. My youngest child was just under two years old. My husband beat me so badly that I spent weeks in the Intensive Care Unit of the military hospital. My jaw was wired together, and I had to use a cane to walk for a couple of years. I had stitches and wounds all over my body. There wasn't any doubt in my mind that this was the last time he would ever do this to me. I had finally concluded that I had to get out … even though he had told me on numerous occasions that he would kill me if I ever left and took the kids away from him.

I had bought a little red Volkswagen that I named Charlie, for some unknown reason, while we were stationed in Europe a few years earlier. After several weeks in the hospital, I loaded it up with my three kids and two Boxer dogs and headed toward Arizona. It was the only home I'd ever known, and my mother was here. I had limited funds and I go into detail in my book about that trip, how I survived this beating, and what it was like starting over with three small children in a small town where the "Tison" name was prevalent and not in a good way.

I didn't know much about racism growing up. The neighborhood I grew up in was quite diversified with just about every race of folks. Our family didn't stand out much except for my father's and brothers' criminal activities bringing the police to our home more frequently than others. All the kids in our neighborhood attended what is now called Ocotillo Elementary School, however, was known then as South School. Only in the seventh grade when we were bused to junior high school north of the tracks, I quickly learned that my friends and I didn't belong most anywhere in the school and that racism was rampart even though racists names weren't quite as common as they are now. Most of us worked in the cafeteria so we could have hot, free lunches. There were no programs then such as there are now. If you worked, you got to eat for free, as simple as that. I personally thought the cafeteria food was on a five-star level, and I didn't even know at the time what a five-star restaurant quality food was; I just knew it was so good, and it was plentiful, unlike home. Going hungry was a frequent memory of growing up. If you have ever gone hungry for any length of time, only then can you have such an appreciation for the quantity of food that was available to us by working in the cafeteria.

Working in the cafeteria was a dead giveaway that we were poor as hell and not like the other kids. I chuckle now in retrospect, like this was the only clue – there were many tell-tale signs of poverty: home haircuts; old, and worn-out, hand-me-down clothes, and shoes. Being apparent to the other kids, and the fact that none of us were ever picked for any sports for many reasons, but mostly because we had after school jobs to get to. The other was our families couldn't afford the specific clothing that was required of the activity, and we surely weren't a part of any clique.

I grew up in this same community where most of their criminal activity took place and ultimately raised my three children here as well. I tolerated those who came against me due to the criminal activities of my father and brothers and my last name being Tison. However, it got increasingly worse when my brother, Gary, escaped from Arizona State Prison in July 1978 with the help of his three sons, and another inmate, Randy Greenwalt. I honestly didn't think it could get any worse, but it did after the escape. It became the largest manhunt in the history of the Southwest and continued for eleven days and ended in a roadblock south of Casa Grande. My nephew, Donnie Joe, was shot in the head and died at the scene, while Ricky, Raymond, and Randy were taken into custody and Gary escaped into the desert. Six innocent people died during their eleven-day rampage.

Although it has been forty plus years since Gary's escape and the killing of six innocent people, and I've watched those who came against me fall over the years. The inhuman treatment from some folks was almost intolerable, simply because I was related, assuming I was bad because some family members was bad, and nothing could have been further from the truth. My mother consistently told me I wasn't guilty of anything because of relationship, but it was difficult thanks to the wrath my family members and I had to endure. As disruptive and dysfunctional as my childhood and teen years were, Gary's escape was the worst of what I had ever experienced by all their actions. It's not right that people treat you horribly because of something that was not your fault, unfortunately, that is the way many are.

As a young girl, my father heard me telling a friend once that I was going to get an education, drive nice cars, and live in a beautiful home. He grabbed me by the shirt, flung me to the ground and said, "What do you think you are going to do, be the fucking President of the United States? You need to get your ass out in the fields and chop cotton or I'm gonna beat your ass." I chuckled to myself because he didn't realize at the time that all he was doing was motivating me to study harder and get out of this environment. Once he threw all my books and schoolwork away after I worked for hours on preparing a book report. I had to explain to my teacher why I needed another book and somehow, he seemed to just know – perhaps he read the newspapers and realized what I dealt with at home. He asked no questions, only went, and got me another book and said, "I'm sure the report you did would have gotten an A, so I'm giving you and A on that assignment." As the years past, it was folks such as this that made me realize there were good people in the world and helped change the course of my life, for they were not all like RC and my brothers. After that, I learned to memorize my homework and anything else I did for school, so if RC threw anything away, it would be in my head.

One day during seventh grade, I stood outside my class-room, under a big tree crying. I had spilled food onto my blouse while working in the cafeteria and trying to get it off with paper towels in the bathroom only made it worse. Mr. Sullivan, my science teacher, walked by and asked me why I was crying, I told him the rich kids were making fun of me because I had food on my blouse. I referred to most anyone who didn't come from the south side of the tracks as "the rich kids."

He said, "You know there is a way out of poverty."

I asked "How?" through tearful eyes.

"Education."

His statement changed my life forever. I was so determined after that to get an education and get out of poverty. Mr. Sullivan died just a few years ago and when I read his obituary in the newspaper, I decided to attend the funeral. My thoughts while sitting through the service were, "Sir, you will never, ever know how you changed my life with your one statement."

Despite what RC said, my mother – out of earshot of RC, of course – always told me to continue to study and get an education, to work hard, be honest, treat others as I wanted to be treated, and life would be good for me. She was right!

While being asked to speak to a group of LDS students years prior about the importance of an education, one ask me "What does success mean to you"? It was an easy and simple answer: *"I can eat meat any day of the week I want, they are never going to turn my power off again for lack of payment, and if I have a flat tire on my truck, I don't have to wait until payday to buy a new one."*

*For all those strong people, who have been through a
lot in life and survived
I am strong because I know weakness,
I am compassionate because I have experienced
suffering,
I am alive because I am a fighter,
I am wise because I've been foolish,
I can laugh because I have known sadness
I can love because I've known loss*

Loving ourselves through the process of owning our story is the bravest thing we'll ever do.

- Brene Brown

Chapter 1
Courtrooms

Sitting in a Superior Court Room in Florence, Arizona, once again for one of my brothers, I was afraid and confused. My mother sat holding hands with her dear friend, Mrs. Leonard, while other friends and relatives from the church, including the minister sat nearby. Everyone was praying, as the jury returned with a verdict for Gary Tison.

This surely was not my mother's first time in front of a judge with a family member. I learned, at the age of 28, my father, RC had chosen a life of crime. In 1937, he robbed a store in Texarkana, Texas, and apparently was not caught for some time; later in the year, he robbed yet another store in McAlester, Oklahoma, this time close to where he lived. The owner of the store as well as numerous customers, recognized him, and he was arrested. RC always thought he was smarter than the average person, and even though he knew the store owner and others recognized him, he felt nobody would say anything bad about him, as he was so well liked. Typical narcissistic behavior.

For mother, many years, and a lifetime of sitting in courtrooms with her husband or sons with their continued criminal activities that lasted each of their lifetimes, it all started in 1937, when she sat on the front row in the courtroom benches for the first time of many. She sat with Gary in her lap, and pregnant with Joe, the first two children of seven, praying and crying, as she always did when one of them got into trouble. Of course, RC told the judge that he had found God, he had realized the error of his ways. According to the court records, he elaborated that "he only wanted to work hard, take care of his family and of course, had made a horrific mistake by committing this crime. He had also found Jesus and his heart was pure." According to records, he explained to the judge that God had forgiven him and asked the judge to do the same and give him another chance.

The judge took pity on him, partly because of his young, pregnant wife sitting on the front row, holding a young son, pregnant with another and was lenient with sentencing, giving him only two years in the state penitentiary for armed robbery. He was released in 1939. Joe, their second son was born while RC was in prison. The judge gave RC a firm warning when released from prison after two years and explicitly told him he never wanted to see him in his courtroom again.

After sentencing, mother moved back with her poor, hardworking farming family. RC's family blamed my mother for what their son had done, never taking responsibility for his behaviors.

Mother told me the stories years later of how RC had desperately looked for work after being released from prison, during what was referred to as the Dust Bowl in and around Durant, Oklahoma, which is where my parents lived. Land was completely stripped of any future hope for farming or anything else, and no money available for construction. Bankers repossessed almost all the land, and farm businesses, supported by the farmers also closed. Soon the bankers basically owned everything, but there was no line of folks to buy back, as farmers were ruined, and farm foremen and workers had no hope of making any sort of a living. To say they were destitute would have been an understatement.

My mother attended numerous Pentecostal tent revivals during these difficult times as other destitute folks, all being offered forgiveness and a new start if only they would give their hearts to Jesus, repent of their sins, and believe. Mother of course, continually prayed RC would attend with her, find Jesus and repent. That never happened; he only got religion when locked up in prison for one thing or another. The old Pentecostal sermons convinced all attendees that if they did not repent, they were damned to hell with no hope for a future. Fire and brimstone type sermons that made you want to run to the front near the pulpit and confess your sins, asking for forgiveness. For hardened men like RC, he not only did not attend with mother but never bought into all this fire and brimstone until he was imprisoned and then each time, got religion and made a vow to walk the straight and narrow. Unfortunately, that only lasted until he was released into society the next time, and he immediately went back to his life of crime.

In late 1939 without RC finding any work whatsoever, he decided to take his young, naive wife, and by now, two sons, Gary, and Joe, and one of my older sisters, while mother was pregnant with yet another child, and head to California. He convinced my mother that jobs were plentiful there, they would make good money and finally have a good life, the life he felt they deserved. They packed up an old Ford truck and headed west. According to the stories my mother shared with me, were very much out of the playbook of John Steinbeck's *The Grapes of Wrath*. Years later, mother rented the movie and had my kids and I watch this with her when they were young and described how similar it was to their relocating to the West.

During this time – the *Dust Bowl* as it was and still is in history referred to – people did not want to leave what they knew as home with relatives and ties to the community, but no choices were given to many of them as there simply was no work. RC had a wife, three kids and another on the way, and now had a prison record, so finding work would be especially hard for him. According to mother, nobody wanted to hire an ex-convict, but now I believe this is just one of many stories RC told her to justify his way of life. However, she always came to his defense.

Dusty roads to California, most roads were paved only in towns as they traveled through, between each town were mostly rocky, dirt roads. Mother told me once that it was so dusty, they had to tie wet clothes around their mouth and nose to keep from choking. Gas was about 15 cents per gallon. According to mother, he tried hard to find a farm job of some sort after the judge had released him on parole in 1939, but during those years of the Great Depression times were hard. Records indicate a long-term drought, fields had dried up and no work for anyone, even some of the most successful farmers were struggling which left little to no work for the farm hands. Durant in the eastern part of the state was hit the hardest. The fields simply dried up and blew away, taking all the nutrients in the soil along as well, nothing left but sand and miles of empty spaces where farmland use to be, and no water to start over again. The drought disrupted many families, especially those poor Okies that worked the fields, causing them to relocate to

Arizona and California. I have always jokingly said, based
on what information I had, was that those Okies with money went onto California, while the poorest of the poor stayed in Arizona and tried to scratch out a living with southern
Arizona farmers.

RC decided to detour onto the southern route as they
came into Arizona, as did others, not imagining the Salt
River Canyon and its treacherous climb. Mother recalled
walking beside the car to lighten the load with her small
children, carrying the youngest though pregnant. Even by
lightening the load, the car constantly overheated and had
to be stopped alongside of the narrow road through the
canyon to allow the car to cool off before attempting again
to reach the top. It was a two-day trip after that to reach the
valley. Mother only took that trip one more time in her life,
and that was with Joe years later to visit Pinetop. She swore
it was day déjà vu for her, even though the roads were
much better, remembering that horrific trip through the
Canyon in the 1940s and vowed to never do it again. To my
knowledge, she did not.

Phoenix at this time was still mostly agricultural, and RC
found a job and they remained there till 1942. As his
restless history indicates, he was ready to move onto the
Promised Land of California, Arvin specifically. He had a
brother, Ben who lived there with his family, Uncle Ben
owned and operated a successful tucking company. He and
my father were nothing alike and his own brother would
not even give him a job. History indicates almost 200,000
migrants came into Kern County. Mother spoke of armed
guards who would patrol and encourage folks to move on,
however most did not have the funds to keep moving and

had no choice but to stay in filthy camps and tents waiting to pick fruit or any other type of farm work they could get, just to feed their families.

Looking back, I often wondered where RC got the money to travel west and start over with his family. After all, he had been released from prison and had not had a job since being paroled; however, knowing his history now, I can only guess that the money used was from some robbery of some sort along the way that he didn't get caught pulling off, perhaps because they were on the road, moving more west each day, and of course he didn't know anyone in the towns they went through, so nobody recognized him. This unfortunately, was the start of many years of transient living to include more children who had yet been born, including myself – California to Arizona, back again and again. We chopped and picked cotton in Arizona and fruit in California, as the seasons changed. I used to envy the kids in school that had lived in one place their entire lives. I could not even begin to relate to that.

Mother always was close to her Dixon family, and they were saddened when she left Oklahoma with such an ir-re-sponsible husband. From the beginning, they considered him no good and begged her not to go. Her parents were a poor farming family, barely scratching out a living, yet honest and God-fearing. RC came from Oklahoma City and her parents always felt he was a city slicker and their daughter deserved better. Her sister, Ozelle despised RC to the day she died, blaming him for the rough life my mother had to endure, and she wasn't wrong. He was exactly as they depicted him, but mother loved him deeply and wouldn't hear of any negativity they offered about her husband.

Before leaving Oklahoma, they made a stop in Oklahoma City to see RC's family. They never liked my mother much and always thought RC married beneath himself, which was absolutely a joke if you had known them both. They tried to convince RC to return mother and the young children to her parents and make the trip without them, telling him he could send for them when he got situated. Mother told me once it was their way of getting rid of her and having RC start a life without her and their children. Unfortunately for my mother, RC would not hear of it, and they immediately left. As sad as it would have been for her at the time for RC to desert her and had to live her with her parents, any life of hers would have been so much better and her sons would not have been influence by RC to become criminals.

During the devastating trip from Oklahoma to Arizona and then eventually onto California, they often slept on the side of the road with my mother cooking over an open campfire. All the time, RC promising her a better life once they reached California. She had told me once how RC used to leave camp to go somewhere that always was important and necessary while she was busy trying to feed the children and prepare for the next day's journey. As always, she did not question him about much, trusting him to do what was right, but she knew he did not know anyone in these towns they were driving through, but as always, she never questioned him. As mother told me about these stories over the years, becoming apparent to me that RC obviously was going off to rob and steal money to continue to their destination. I once asked her why she did not question where he was going or what he was doing when he left their camp, and she only said that "He always seemed to know what he was doing, and I was too busy trying to cook a meal out in the middle of nowhere, wash clothes in a bucket, and take care of young kids."

Their destination was Bakersfield after leaving Arizona to follow RC's dream to California. They ended up in a Federal Government Camp in Arvin, Calif., which is ultimately where I was born. The government provided slabs for tents to be set up, and each site had a cook stove and running water. According to my mother, it was an improvement from sleeping and camping on the side of the road on that long, dusty road on U.S. Hwy. 66 from Oklahoma.

This camp was considered a government rescue center for distressed migrant workers fleeing the Oklahoma Dust Bowl, during the Great Depression. To this day, the camp still aids migrant workers. Most migrants went from farm to farm looking for work, they came from Texas, Arkansas, Missouri and, of course, Oklahoma Dust Bowl.

Housing for workers consisted of either squatter camps (tents pitched by the side of the road) or camps established by the farmers and growers. Because of the lack of hygiene and security that these types of camps offered, the FSA built labor camps consisting of permanent buildings with running water, schools, libraries, camp stores and other amenities that families needed. The FSA also went so far as to help people locate work. The Arvin Federal Government Camp plays an important part of California's history, helping those escape the Dust Bowl. Unfortunately, those who lived and worked in those camps were discriminated against by the local population. They were considered Okies, and the locals did not want them there – however, the farmers and growers did, as they needed the labors, and the camps grew. I was born at home, and my birth certificate reads, "Arvin California Federal Government Cotton Camp" as the address.

The name of the camp eventually was changed to Sunset Labor Camp. The camp was renamed by judge Lovejoy due to the beautiful sunsets – ironically renamed by a judge considering infamous Gary's criminal history started in this camp.

RC managed to land a good foreman's job that came with a nice house and all the amenities afforded a foreman. My second older sister were born, then Larry and myself, the younger sister came later. My older sisters remember a beautiful swimming pool in the labor camp they could use anytime and, of course, their own church right there in the camp. Mother was very content there according to the stories she told me over the years. She once told me she felt her family was wrong about RC and that he was finally taking good care of his family and she felt fortunate to have a nice home and what she considered a good life. She was such a humble, grateful Lady, it did not take much to make her happy. Always being a God-fearing woman and taking her children to church, she continued this path. Gary was 14 years old and active in the church they attended, he had a beautiful voice, loved to sing, and even preached at times to the youth. As time passed, RC wanted Gary working with him and not spending so much time at the church. As always, RC ruled the roost, and nobody came against him. During this time, it was when Gary learned another way of life, a life of criminal activity and from his own father. He became more like RC that the Christian son mother was trying to raise.

Gary soon learned to defend himself from the scorn of locals, who referred to migrants as filthy Okies who needed to go home. Little did the locals know or care that there was no home to return too and no money to move on. At a young age, Gary used his fighting skills to survive, dropping out of school and working for our father to help support the family.

Gary's first run-in with the law was for robbing a store. He had told himself if he could get enough money together, he could convince mother to take her children and leave RC and give us a better life. He knew at a young age that RC was no good, and he watched him cheat and lie his way through each day. However, mother would never agree to do so. She had unconditional love for RC, putting him over the best interest of her children. As Gary was a juvenile, the judge gave him probation for robbing that store.

RC got hurt in a farm accident shortly thereafter and was hospitalized for months. Gary drove a tractor, which paid more than regular farm work, and had paid off so many of the family's debts, including the local camp store where credit was issued. However, when RC got out of the hospital, the first thing he did was purchase a 1951 Ford and put them right back into debt. My mother was furious, as were Gary and Joe, since they had worked to take care of mother and all of us while RC was lying in a hospital bed. RC always said, "it's important to look successful even if you aren't." I never quite understood that, especially as it was literally taking food out of the mouths of his children.

There was no reasoning with RC on his lifestyle. Gary and Joe could not convince mother to stand up to him, so they stole a new Chevy from a local car dealer in Arvin and took a joy ride to Arizona. Right outside of Bakersfield, they robbed a gas station for less than $50 and a tank of gas, then they stole the owner's gun. Mother shared with me many times over the years that she wished she had left with them when they ask, before giving up, stealing a car, and leaving for Arizona. She had shared with me that she believed they would have both worked hard and would have taken care of her and us younger siblings. She knew in her heart that her boys would have taken a different path in life without RC to corrupt them.

When arriving in Casa Grande, Arizona, Gary, and Joe stole a license plate from another vehicle and headed toward Mammoth, where they robbed a local store. Pinal County Sheriff's Department received the notification about the robbery and the two were located near the town of Winkelman, a pursuit of their vehicle ended with their being run off the road by sheriff's deputies and arrested. Gary was 19 and Joe 16. Gary was sentenced to seven to ten years in Arizona State Prison and Joe placed on probation due to his age, and as the judge felt he had been influenced by his older brother, Gary.

Mother wanted to be with her son, Gary, and be there for him when he went to court, and RC was restless again, so we packed up whatever little bit we owned and relocated to Arizona.

Mother had told me that RC always worked as a farm foreman. He was great at it, and one of those people who could throw seeds in the ground while just passing by, and they grew into something wonderful. She called it a God-given talent; unfortunately, he liked the fast money and never held a job for any length of time. Mother explained to me years later that RC was restless and always needing to move on to something better. As I looked back in retrospect growing up, with mother sharing stories of their life, became apparent to me that he had been that way his entire life.

During these hard times, mother turn to God and the Pentecostal Church for comfort and support .... while my father continued his life of crime. When returning to Casa Grande, she immediately started attending the Pentecostal Church of God at Fifth and Lincoln Street in Casa Grande and remained with that church for many years.

Gary served a couple of years and was released on parole for the theft of the car he had stolen in California and drove to Arizona. Gary's role model unfortunately was RC, a hard-drinking father who was constantly in and out of prisons himself starting in 1937. Following in his father's footsteps to prison hardened Gary early. Gary approached life through a lens of aggression and violence. Although highly intelligent, he dropped out of school in the tenth grade and followed his father's example of antagonism with the law.

In 1955, when Gary was 20, we were living in Casa Grande, south of Phoenix, and Gary was in prison again, this time for armed robbery. A family member befriended Dorothy Stanford, a shy and devout Christian girl, at the Glad Tidings Pentecostal Church. Dorothy was invited to join in for those ritual family prison visits on Sunday to see Gary. Dorothy immediately fell in love with this handsome prisoner whom she saw as kind, polite, charming, and intelligent. To this naive girl, he seemed the perfect man except he had made a couple mistakes and was serving time in prison. He looked like anything but a criminal to her.

As if it could not get any worse in July 1957, after Gary's release from prison again, RC informed us that Gary and Dorothy were going to be moving into one of the houses on the farm, right near us. Gary and Dorothy were married in October 1957 shortly after his release on parole in September. They had their first son, Donnie Joe, on January 1 after his release, and Ricky and Raymond came shorts periods after that. The fact that Donnie Joe was born so soon after his release confirmed what I thought might have been going on in the bathroom of the prison visiting rooms, however being such a young girl, I had thought they were just kissing and making out, never realizing at the time, that they were having sex. I was not the smartest kid on the block, as had been pointed out to me many times by my father and brothers, but I knew a pregnancy lasted nine months.

Eddie Hoyt had also given Gary a job, he even went so far as to write the parole board a letter of such promise, as requested by Dorothy, to help get him released. Gary terrified me, as I had always been afraid of him; he was extremely mean, cruel, and cared only for himself. Now, according to our father, he was going to live right next door. He was without a doubt a sociopath with psychotic tendencies. He took the job for Eddie Hoyt upon his release from prison, and the house near ours was part of the job.

In the beginning, I would always run and hide if I saw him coming and made sure I kept my distance from him. However, in my young, inquisitive mind, I knew he and RC were working on some scheme to get rich quick, rip someone off, or even murder someone to get what they wanted.

I watched and listened until mother caught me one day, told me to stay away, and to mind my own business. I could not help but laugh, thinking "This is my business because whatever they do will affect us all." Gary told me once that if I ever got into his way, or repeated anything I had heard, he would bury me with one of the pieces of equipment on the farm, and nobody would even miss me. I used to lay awake nights and worry about this. After that, I kept my distance or at least was more careful not to let them catch me listening in on them and their schemes.

My brother, Larry, and I worked on the farm for my father. We were never paid, just did whatever work he assigned to us. If we did not do it well, we got the crap beat out of us, so it was easier to just do the work and do it as well as we could. Larry and I used to get left out in fields near the cemetery to irrigate and/or chop weeds out of cotton. I used to be so afraid to be this close to the cemetery, especially after dark, and would beg RC to pick us up before it got dark. Once the ditch broke and irrigation water got away from us. When he showed up around dusk, the truck was still moving when he jumped out of it and started cussing at us about how stupid we were. Now keep in mind, he had been off drinking and with some women all afternoon, and we were doing his job, but according to him, not good enough considering there was water everywhere. My God, we were kids and doing a man's job every day in the fields. I yelled at Larry to run, but he was frozen and just stood there while RC beat him. I ran, I ran like a deer nearly four miles to our place on Selma Highway because I knew if I just got to the house and hid long enough, he would get past his anger and probably wouldn't beat me nearly as bad, possibly not at all. I did not eat dinner that night because I was still hiding out in the equipment yard hoping he would go to bed, and I could sneak in. When I did finally go inside, I heard Larry crying from the whips on his back from the irrigation hose that RC had beaten him with. I snuck into the bathroom to find something to put on them to help ease the pain. He asked why I had not gotten beat and I told him I'd run home and hid, and next time; he should run too.

When the movie Forrest Gump – "Run Forrest Run" came out years later, I could honestly relate to him and his need to run. As I watched this movie for the first time, it took me back to an extremely unhappy time in my life. "Fight or flight" takes on new meaning when you grow up with this type behaviors going on around you and I always knew I could not fight RC, as the repercussions would have been worse if I fought back. He would have possibly beaten me to death and buried me like Gary promised to do if I got into his way. Mother would always give us a quart of water to take to the fields with us. A few times RC simply said, "you don't need that you spoiled babies, drink out of the damn ditch" as he pulled the quart of water from our hands and threw onto the floorboard of his truck. I learned to take a clean cloth with me so I could filter the water from the ditch before drinking it. Many years later I originated and operated a water treatment business and chuckled at knowing about water purification years ago when having to drink canal ditch water.

For a while, and according to mother, Gary appeared to try to be a good husband and father, although, like his father, he simply could not keep a job long and resisted authority in its entirety. Like RC, nothing ever lasted long, as he was always looking for the quick money. He admitted in a later interview with a psychiatrist that "I'm never going to be that normal husband and father, I'm always the smartest person in the room with a higher IQ than anyone else," which he probably was, but he used his God-given talents of intelligence to conduct criminal activity rather than for something productive. He, like RC, loved the life of crime. He loved Dorothy and his sons, but not enough to give up the life of crime, always thinking he would succeed this time and not get caught. As I looked back, I realized that Dorothy was always aware of what Gary was doing, also wanting a better life for herself and sons, any way she could get it, and supported any decisions he made ... criminal and otherwise.

Gary and RC had concocted numerous crimes but were not caught until Gary went on a couple of weeks crime spree, armed robbery and ultimately stealing guns from the National Guard Armory in Casa Grande, where people knew him. He thought like RC did in 1937 – that people simply would not report him or identify him either out of friendship or fear. His intent apparently was to get the guns into Mexico before he would be caught, sell them off and, of course, lie his way out of it by not being the person they thought he was, with the witnesses making a mistake in identity, and, of course, RC swearing he was working on the farm the entire day. Of course, my opinion was always that criminals either were not too smart or thought they were smarter than anyone else, ultimately always getting caught.

Gary was arrested right in front of the entire family right outside the farmhouse we lived in, and I remember think-ing how small and weak he looked, not the tough guy he always tried to project himself as. I remember thinking that it was probably the first time I had *not* been afraid of him but then of, course, there were numerous cops there, and he was handcuffed face down in the dirt. You can't look too tough when surrounded by police officers, handcuffed, and thrown to the ground. I remember the saddened look in my mother's eyes, as they hauled yet another member of her family away to jail … again.

I feared he would come to us for help, and nobody wanted to help him. If I remember correctly, Gary never "asks" anything; he spoke and expected results. The two nights he was on the loose, I slept in the barn thinking he would not come in there and felt as safe as a young girl could feel with him on the run. I laughingly remember finding a big stick to protect myself, like that would make a difference with someone like Gary, but it made me feel safer.

When captured after two days on the run, the prosecuting attorney asked Gary to be evaluated to make sure he was mentally stable enough to stand trial. I assumed he desperately wanted to prosecute him and wanting to make sure all his bases was covered. The psychiatrist who examined him stated among other things in his report that "Gary Tison is impressed with being dangerous. He wants others to fear him." As I recall for the first time, someone finally concluded that this man was a danger to others and a threat to society. Hell, I could have told them that years ago, but nobody asked me. And yet, another Mental Health Psychiatrist who worked for the State of Arizona evaluated Gary and determined that in his self-image considered himself dangerous, diagnosing him as having a psychopathic personality. And yet another psychiatrist once diagnosed Gary as being criminally insane, along with other labels nobody would ever want attached to their names. Crime had been so embedded into my brothers from our father, RC, so deeply that it was a way of life, accepted by each one of them with no intent of changing.

In 1962, Gary was once again arrested, this time for passing a bad check for $50. His statement to the judge was one we had all heard numerous times before. "I made a mistake, Your Honor. I have since given my life to the Lord and just want to work hard and take care of my family." In my opinion, good thing they all had different judges, otherwise the judge would have known this line by heart considering how many times they had all been in court and consistently used the same statement.

Considering his criminal history, I doubt the judge would have ever been so lenient had the truck stop owner, Doug Ballard, agreed to not pursue charges after Joe paid him the $50 back. Doug and our brother, Joe, had grown up together, being friends since childhood which is most likely why he choose to drop the charges against Gary, mostly because Joe probably asked him too. I always questioned Doug's morality and integrity based on the fact he and Joe were such good friends, based on the ole' adage of "birds of a feather." I knew what Joe was, and that he was a seasoned criminal and deep into the Cartel and running drugs. Doug never did me any harm, and as I became older and raising my children in Casa Grande, he tried on numerous occasions to befriend me. Like my father and brothers, I wanted nothing to do with him. He took it personal, which he should have, and said some unkind things to me. I shrugged it off and walked away, saying "It's my choice, and I choose not to associate with you."

Once again, Gary was released from prison on parole and only took him about ten months to end up back in prison, perhaps sooner, but it took ten months for him to get caught this time. Gary was heavily involved in smuggling deals in Mexico with cattle and farm machinery. According to the stories I was told, he doubled-crossed his partners, who were also crooks, and they reported him, causing yet another arrest. By September 1963, Gary had been arrested again due to a parole violation and was also convicted on the other charges, which included smuggling. His was sentenced to serve consecutive sentences of his parole as well as the new charges. There appeared to be no future for Dorothy and her boys, however, she did not give up. Her devotion went much deeper than anyone could have even guessed. She continued to stand behind him, and worst, she would continue to drag her three young sons to the prison every Sunday to visit their father. He took this opportunity to brainwash and convince them he had done nothing wrong; the system was broken, and law enforcement just had it in him for him. Dorothy and the boys all bought into it – except for Donnie Joe, the oldest. He had a good head on his shoulders and knew Gary was blowing smoke as he got older, but nobody disrespected Gary ever or paid a terrible price for it. Donnie Joe kept his thoughts to himself, even though he was pressured to continue those Sunday visits, but he also knew, he was going to do something good with his life. After the Marines, he immediately enrolled at Central Arizona College and was planning to attend North Arizona University using his VA benefits, with a future in criminal justice. Unfortunately, that never happened for him, as his life was cut short by being sucked into the escape that Gary and Dorothy planned to use their sons to carry out in 1978.

Chapter 2
Gary and Dorothy
Moving Next Door to Us

Growing up, we always had a huge garden which RC planted and us girls, along with our mother, always canned all the goodies for winter months. RC made it abundantly clear every year, that he would plant the garden once we got the rows or mounds ready and would only plant, do no hoeing, chopping or anything else once the seeds were planted. I remember this is how it was for so long, that it seemed natural. If he happened to see weeds amongst the plants or perhaps was not getting enough water when he checked it, we'd get beat to the inch of our lives. The gardens got lots of attention, it was just easier than being beat, cussed and yelled at.

I've always professed that if you live abnormally long enough, it becomes normal and for us, this was normal. Studying psychology, I look back in retrospect and realized just how abnormal our childhood was, however what choice did we have!? We were too young to go out on our own, and didn't know about Child Protective Services, even if there was one in existence at that time, you didn't dare tell anyone even at church or school because the ramifications would have been severe once RC learned of it.

One of the few advantages of living on this farm was it had a circular driveway and one of my sisters learn to drive at 15 years old. She would drive that old broken-down Jeep around the equipment yard and occasionally let me ride with her. She was always RC's favorite, so he kept the Jeep running and kept fuel in it for her. We must have put a million miles on that Jeep going only around the equipment yard.

Larry and I used to walk out to the ditch bank right off the Old Tucson Highway (now known as Jimmy Kerr Boulevard) to catch the school bus on the corner of Selma Highway. There were several kids from the area who waited with us. In the winter months it was so cold. We found an old barrel and made every kid bring wood they found on their way so we could stay warm while waiting for the school bus. Unlike today when their schedules are more punctual, we often waited an hour or more for the bus to pick us up. However, we would much rather wait than take the chance on missing the bus, as RC will work the hell out of you if you happen to miss it, and he had you for a day. I suppose I was not too smart because I could never figure out how Larry got the damn thing started so quick until I saw him throw some gas on it which he had siphoned out of RC's truck. We didn't smell exactly fresh when arriving at school, but we also didn't freeze waiting either. Not smelling good seemed secondary to the alternative of freezing or working for RC.

We had a pig, for butchering purposes since we were not allowed pets, so I only went out to feed and water it, careful to not make it a pet, as I knew it would not be around long. One day it got out of its pen as one of us left the gate open. Gary shot the pig, as it ran around the house, then hung it from my swing to let it bleed out for butchering. I was devastated as that swing was my solitude and a place for me to go when it got so bad inside. It hung from a huge old tree, and I felt I could almost reach the stars when swinging with its long, sturdy ropes. It was built by one of the farm hands who took pity on me and my kid sister. I cried myself to sleep that night, not sure if for the pig or the loss of my swing, perhaps both, but I remember feeling sad and helpless.

A week or so later, mother had made some yeast rolls to take the minister of our church. While loading other items, she sat them in the back seat of our old car and left the door open while running back inside. An old stray dog got into the car and ate the rolls. Mother was crying, as she had worked so hard and was such a giving person, especially to our minister and family. Gary walked up and shot the dog then looked at Larry and me and said, "Clean this shit up and bury the SOB." Oh, crap how were we supposed to do that!? It was a bloody mess. I helped Larry, and we loaded the dead dog into a box with a shovel, dragged the box away from the house, dug a hole, and buried it. I was sad the dog got shot, sad my mother's rolls were all eaten, but the most traumatizing fact was that Gary just walked up, shot the dog, and had absolutely no remorse. I could not help but wonder how many people he had done this to. I did not sleep for days, and it ultimately made me even more afraid of him than I already was.

After serving another short prison sentence, Gary was yet again released from prison, but only took a few months for him to end up back in crime.

My mother, Dorothy, numerous members of our family, and all those good ol' Pentecostals were sitting in Superior

Court in Florence in front of yet another judge. Nobody ever had anyone watch their children for such devastating events; they would just drag us along and allow us to be traumatized by things we did not understand or have any control over. And of course, some of those ol' Pentecostals weren't about to miss this show so they'd have firsthand gossip to tell everyone who would listen. I felt our Minister and Mrs. Leonard genuinely cared about my mother and were there for prayer and support. Numerous others, in my opinion, were there simply to have firsthand gossip to spread.

Right at the beginning of January 1963, Gary was sentenced to 25-30 years in Arizona State Prison. Once again, everyone was devastated that a jury of twelve honest, hardworking people could find him guilty and return him to prison for such a long period of time; after all, he had a wife and children. However, what I saw was so did the good people he victimized but nobody on our side of the courtroom was taking this into consideration.

Dorothy and her small sons had moved back in with her parents who lived on Trekell Road where they operated a gas station and tire repair right next door to their house. Her parents continued to tell her that Gary was no good and that she should divorce him and start a new life. Unfortunately, what they did not know was it was too late, she was already so much like Gary and would continue her weekly visits to the prison with her small children in tow, to be with him. He had the same type of emotional hold on her that RC had on our mother. They loved these men unconditionally and were going to stand behind them no matter what, and nobody, not even their children's best interest, was going to change that.

I wasn't allowed to cuss in any form, as mother would have given me a whipping I wouldn't soon forget, however I sat in that courtroom thinking "Holy shit, what is wrong with these people? He broke the law, hurt people, took their belongings, and was going to sell all these guns in Mexico where guns are illegal to own. Am I the only one in this courtroom besides the judge and jury who felt he was guilty?" I kept my mouth shut and did not even asked questions, which was unusual for me.

I never really understood if mother was a mentor to Dorothy to "Stand by Your Man" type lifestyle or if they just truly took her marriage vows seriously enough to subject her sons to prison visits as our mother had done to us.

I once felt every man should have a woman who was as dedicated to them as mother was to RC and Dorothy to Gary. Only secondary to their marriage vows were their religion and dedication to the church, especially my mother.

Dorothy and mother inundated the parole board with letters pleading hardship and convinced others to write on Gary's behalf – those who did write letters, wrote more out of sympathy to Dorothy and the boys and mother, than any belief in Gary's rectitude. Dorothy did what women married to Tison men did ... started correspondence with parole boards, judges, future employers for them, anyone who would listen. Women in Tison men's lives were always convinced their men got a raw deal and determined to have them set free again .... unfortunately, as their history shows, only to have them return to crime again and again.

One such letter I found in the archives was written to the parole board after Gary was first sent to prison when he and Joe had stolen a car years earlier in Arvin, California and came to Arizona when Gary was only 18 and Joe 16:

> Dear Members of the Arizona State parole board:
>
> My husband and I would like to arrange a meeting with you to discuss our son, Gary's release. My husband cannot find work here in Arizona and we would like very much to go back to California, but I know you will understand why we can't leave without Gary. We feel we should stand by him as he is so young. He can make a decent life for himself and help others as well. That is why we must stand by him. Don't you feel like giving him another chance? We could put both our girls back in school if we were in California. So, when you can see us, would you please let us know? We would appreciate it very much.
>
> Mr. and Mrs. RC Tison

This was one of the first of many letters written on behalf of Gary after his first time in Arizona State Prison. However, between mother and Dorothy, many letters were written over the years to parole boards, prison officials, and anyone else they felt could help obtaining Gary's release.

The parole board commuted his sentence, and he was released within a year. Not lasting long though, as he and RC did not get along but together were scamming new ways to get rich quick. Gary, like his father, always thought he was too smart to do farm work for low wages.

RC's job at the Hoyt Farms did not last too long after Gary went back to prison, but then he never kept a job long, and that was always someone else's fault. So, we moved on. This time we got to live in town on Center Street, right next door to where Heritage House of Flowers eventually was and now Domino's Pizza. Boy was I ever excited. I could walk to downtown and visit my one dear friend, Sissy. I could also clean houses for folks, babysit, and buy some decent clothes. And most important .... I did not have to work for RC on the farm or to be subject to his verbal, physical and sexual abuse. That was the best of it all!

Chapter 3
Gary's Sentencing for Escape/Killing Prison Guard

In 1964, Gary was once again back in prison. His parole was revoked on the previous charges, and in April he was sent back to jail, awaiting trial for all the charges. He was facing a twenty-five-year prison sentence. He served only a few years of his sentence for the previous crimes when he was paroled yet again, only to almost immediately start back into criminal activity. He and our father concocted a scheme to smuggle farm equipment into Mexico, along with four other men in our community. Gary apparently had pocketed some of the bribe money, and the other partners turned him in, protecting themselves but determined to put him back in prison for double-crossing them. Our father was a coward of a man, and had always big plans, but was usually in the sidelines to ensure he did not get caught. I often wondered what kind of a father would throw their own son under the bus when it came down to the wire. When living on the Hoyt Farm, I often heard he and Gary talking about their big plan; what RC didn't count on was Gary pocketing some of the bribe money and their partners turning him in.

When Gary was arrested, I thought I'd choke when listening to RC tell the police, yet again, that he was disappointed as he had gotten Gary this good farm job after he was paroled and now, he had gone and screwed up again. I remembered him saying this almost verbatim in 1962 when Gary was being arrested, when all the time he was up to his neck in the same crime spree Gary was involved in. I remember walking on the ditch bank for miles wondering how "life" for us was so pitiful. As usual, I wondered why my father and brothers could not just work like everyone else and have some normality in our lives. At an early age, I was determined to get an education, work hard and never do anything illegal. I had extremely heavy thoughts for a kid my age. I often felt there was no childhood for us kids .... just survival from abuse and public scrutiny.

Gary was arrested and placed into Pinal County Jail and, of course, it was front page news, probably television as well but we did not have one, so I had no way of knowing. Months passed before his trial date, and as always, mother dragged us kids to the courtroom to be traumatized once again. At a young age, I could tell you how many steps there were in the big old county courthouse, and every detail of the building and just how many trees were in the park area in the front, indicating I had been there with my mother far too many times and found myself emotionally detaching by studying the structure of the building. By focusing on the structure and landscaping took my mind off why we were there and the nightmare, shame, and drama around us.

A judge had told Gary and his attorney to stand for sentencing, and as in all other court proceedings I had been through, I remember hearing the same rehearsed statement about "making a mistake, doing good, working hard, and giving his life to Jesus." I had heard it far too many times from my father and brothers just before a judge pronounced sentence, only this time, the judge was not buying it. He told Gary his parole was revoked and carried an original sentence of twenty-five years. As Gary was led from the courtroom, his wife, Dorothy ran up to him to give him a hug. Prison Guard Jim Stiner pushed her away, informing her she could not have any contact with the prisoner but could see him once he was processed back into the prison. Unfortunately, what the prison guard didn't know was that she had already slipped him a gun and told him where she had stashed a car and clothing for him.

As he was being driven to Arizona State Prison, he pulled the gun Dorothy had given him on the Transport Guard and told him to exit onto a farm road. They ultimately ended up near an irrigation ditch near La Palma, just south of Coolidge. Gary shot him in the chest three times and left to pick up the vehicle and clothing Dorothy had told him about at an abandoned house on the outskirts of Casa Grande. I can only imagine the terror in the heart of this man, knowing Gary's history of violence. I grieved for this man and other victims of Gary's for years, still do. It has been forty plus years, and I still have nightmares when I allow myself to think about the horrific things the men in our family have done.

Gary apparently wandered around Casa Grande for a few days prior to taking a station wagon from a local woman who had a child with her, as she was coming into Casa Grande. Law enforcement learned later that he had entered a house on the west side of town, took food from the kitchen, and held up there for a while in their outside laundry room. It was only later the residents realized it was Gary, and the owners felt blessed, and righteously so, that he hadn't contacted them or hurt them in some way. They were out of town when he entered their kitchen for food, according to a news release. Law enforcement knew it was him from the prison clothing he left behind.

Gary continued to evade law enforcement for a couple days, and everyone in the county, especially here in Casa Grande, was terrified they would come upon him, including myself and other members of my family. I remember folks saying they were carrying weapons, even those who normally did not. Fear swept over the county and state due to his reputation. I never quite understood why when my father or brothers did something terribly wrong, they always hovered around the same town. I always thought that if I were going to be a criminal, not that I ever was, I'd high tail it out of this town, state and possible even the country, never to be seen again. However, no one ever accused them of being too smart.

The woman with her child had reported Gary had taken her station wagon at gunpoint and every officer in the county and state was looking for this vehicle. He was located by a local policeman who was pursuing him in his patrol car. He radioed it in, and within minutes, numerous police officers, sheriff's deputies, and state police were in the area. Gary jumped out of the vehicle he had stolen, ran into a backyard on Lehmberg Avenue, and a gun battle ensued. He was hiding behind the owner's swimming pool pump and continued to fire at officers. One of the officers fired a shot that knocked off his cowboy hat, and he surrendered at that point.

The day Gary was captured, I was walking home from school and was feeling good about life. I had cleaned a couple of houses, babysat, and earned enough money to buy new clothes and maybe even, without mother's permission, get a professional haircut. My grades in school were exceptionally good even though I took a lot of crap from other kids due to my family; it was all still good in my opinion. As I turned around the corner onto Center Street walking home from school, I saw police cars everywhere along the street in front of our house, I thought "Oh shit, here we go again. I wonder which one it was this time." Never in my wildest dreams did I imagine Gary had killed a prison guard and there was a massive manhunt for him. I realized at that moment why school had been let out early. I had not stuck around for the details of why, just left as I usually did right after school.

Once I learned of this murder, I knew I could not go back to high school. I knew in my heart it would be worse than any other crimes my father or brothers had committed. I knew in my heart that I had to leave Casa Grande, but at such a young age, I did not have many options. I had an older sister who lived in Corcoran, Calif., and within a few days my mother had put me on a Greyhound Bus to live with her and go to school. My education was desperately important to me, remembering what the seventh-grade teacher, Mr. Sullivan had told me about education being the way out of poverty. I wanted an education more than anything I could possibly imagine, whether it be in California, Arizona, I simply did not care ... I just wanted it.

I never quite understood why mother thought the whole damn clan be there for Gary, RC, or other brothers when they went to court, however she insisted I get on a bus and return for the trial. I was just a kid, and I could have cared less – he killed a man and, in my heart, felt he should be put to death himself, an "eye for an eye" adage, except I would have never said that out loud or would have been punished severely. It is not like we hadn't been in a courtroom before; however, I was missing school, and that was important to me.

So once again, sitting in a courtroom in Florence, Arizona, with her son, Gary, the same scenario, just years later and her son, not her husband this time. The judge asked the jury if they had reached a verdict, and they had. The jury foreman read the verdict, "This jury unanimously finds Gary Tison guilty of murder in the first degree."

The judge quickly replied, "Do you have anything you want to say before sentence is passed?"

As members of this family had heard numerous times before almost verbatim from brothers as well as our father, "Judge, I have made a mistake and was taught different than that by my mother. However, God has forgiven me, and I intend to live for the Lord the rest of my life. When I get out, I intend to go straight, attend church regularly, and live for the Lord."

I personally was always amazed at how they all got religion as soon as they got caught and locked up and quickly forgot about the good Lord as soon as they returned to society. The judge believed this about as much as I did. He immediately stated, "This court finds Gary Tison guilty of murder in the first degree and sentences him to the Arizona State Penitentiary for two life sentences for the death of Jim Steiner."

My mother collapsed, as her friends helped her out of the courtroom into the large old courtyard under a palm tree where she was able to sit and gain some composure. Everyone had an opinion on the jury, the judge, and of course, my brother, Gary. Why were they all finding it so hard to believe this jury of twelve honest citizens found him guilty of murder? Hell, he admitted to killing a prison guard. Shot him in the chest three times after holding him hostage, as he escaped from the same courtroom only months before. I always felt like I had missed something, somewhere. Was I the only one, other than the jury and judge, who knew he was guilty? If he had to escape, I kept thinking, why couldn't he have just left this guard in the desert to find his way for someone to help him, why did he have to kill him? My heart went out to his family and friends who were also in the courtroom during the trail. You could see the pain in their eyes over the loss of a loved one. In my young mind, I pondered this for years and personally had no sympathy for his sentencing and felt someone who killed another person, should be imprisoned forever, or put to death, ensuring they could never again hurt an innocent person(s). I am sure the prison officials who were terminated years later over their lack of security with such a violent prisoner, would agree with me now after Gary's 1978 escape.

After Gary's sentencing to two consecutive life sentences, in my quest to get answers – which was pretty normal for me since I had always been inquisitive and wanting to understand things –I had asked my mother, while we were standing under a tree in the courthouse yard, and in the softest and kindest voice I could muster, "If this is all so terrible, why does he keep breaking the law, and why did he have to kill that guard? He didn't do anything to him except take him to court like his boss had told him to do."

My mother slapped me across the face. "This is your brother, show some respect."

All I wanted was an honest answer and did not feel I had asked too much. Apparently, I had. A lot of thoughts about Gary came to mind; unfortunately for my mother, "respect" was definitely not what I was feeling for Gary, more like total and absolute contempt and hatred. I knew that we as a family were going to reap his actions for years to come by anyone who knew we were related... and the worst was yet to come in 1978 when he once again escaped from Arizona State Prison and killed six innocent people.

Standing in this courtyard under the old palm trees, and sitting in this courtroom, as well as others were not strange for our mother; she had been in many courtrooms with not only Gary, but the other brothers, Joe, Larry, and our father as well.

Gary's sons idolized him, and to this day, the two serving life sentences in Arizona State Prison still believe he was framed and shot this guard in self-defense. He had a tremendous hold on them emotionally, and they believed anything he told them. God only knows the story he told them about his escape and killing the prison guard. In his narcissistic mind, he believed his own lies. In my opinion, if a person tells themselves something long enough, they start believing it. It is called being a pathological liar, and he was surely that, just like our father, RC.

During the first part of his time back in prison, Gary became the editor of the prison newspaper. In so many of his articles, he praised Warden Cardwell for all he was doing for the prisoners, tight security, budgets, etc. He even went so far as to praise him for his excellent job of protecting the public from criminals and their rehabilitation. He won the approval of the warden and appeared to being rehabilitated, however, if Warden Cardwell had ever read any of the mental health reports done on Gary, he would have known what a sociopath he was and that he was being conned ... It worked for Gary, only three years after he was sentenced for killing Jim Steiner, he was transferred from maximum security to a medium security area in the annex outside the gray walls, which is where he ultimately escaped again. The next few years were spent with Gary planning his escape with the help of his wife and sons on their regular Sunday visits. The visiting area resembled that of a park area, and security was more relaxed than that inside the walls. Gary never should have been reassigned to this minimum-security area, and according to archives, even other prison officials, knowing Gary was a hardened criminal who was never going to be rehabilitated, questioned this decision by the warden. The decision to do this ultimately cost six innocent people their lives.

Gary had three previous escape attempts and was known for his violent behaviors within the prison. Other prisoners and even guards feared him. He was not even subject to the regular shake downs for contraband that other prisoners had to succumb too. He wore cowboy boots rather than regulatory shoes for prisoners and was commonly known to carry a small gun in his boot.

Warden Cardwell was fired after Gary's last escape, as it was apparent to everyone except himself, that Gary should have remained in maximum security, never being allowed to go into the minimum-security annex. The adage that "flattery will get you everywhere" surely worked for Gary with all his praise in the prison newspaper about what a great warden they had at Arizona State Prison, his security and safety of the prisoners. Numerous interviews were given to the Arizona Republic about the warden and his approval to transfer Gary to the Minimum-Security area, even other officials at the prison questioned this decision, but ultimately, he approved it and Gary was transferred.

I was living in Germany at the time with my then husband and two sons, we were military dependents, and I was finally outside the gossip and stares of those who knew I was related to my father or brothers. My sons were too young to know about any of this, and I surely did not tell anyone as it was like being out from under a black cloud, living what I finally thought was a normal life without the stigma that went along with being a Tison. My mother and I wrote regularly, and she had told me about this transfer to the minimum-security area. My first thoughts were "Who the hell decided this with his history of violence and three previous escape attempts?" We didn't have Internet back then, but I did go onto the base from time to time and read newspapers and mother sent me clippings from the Arizona Republic. To say I was astonished by the transfer was an understatement, but as always, I did not share my thoughts with my mother on those few phone calls we had.

I had finally made the decision to leave my abusive husband after returning from Germany. I wasn't sure how or when I could safely get away from him, however the decision was made while living in Key West, Fla., our last duty station, after the last and almost fatal beating from him. I should have known just from history that I should have picked anywhere in the world except Casa Grande, Arizona. However, my mother lived here along with numerous other relatives, and it was "Home" for me and starting over with by now, three small children, I felt safe being around my mother and knew she would help me with my children. Had I had any inclination Gary would escape in the next few years or that Joe would continue his transportation of narcotics from Mexico, or Larry to run Chop Shops, my decision to return here would have been different.

That adage of *Hindsight is 20/20* surely applied to me over the years after returning to my hometown. I looked at my three beautiful children and wondered a hundred times why I had chosen to bring them back to this town and subject them to the scrutiny I had experienced as a child ... simply because I was related to the wrong family.

Gary was only in Pinal County Jail a couple of days when he somehow or another escaped and robbed a local store in Florence. He was only free for a couple of days when found, arrested, and was placed into a more secure area to prevent another escape. However, the terror was great for many, including my family, as he was already known to be dangerous and now, desperate and on the run.

Chapter 4
Dorothy's Move
to California

Going back a few years, after one of Gary's many prison sentences, Dorothy's family finally convinced her that she needed to take the boys and move away and start a new life without Gary. Up to that point, Dorothy had never seriously listened when her family and friends told her to leave Gary for good and start over. But without the slimmest hope that Gary would ever be released, she had to consider what was best for her boys. She quit her job, pulled the boys out of school, and moved to Wilmington, Calif., where several of us were living at the time.

To my surprise, my father and brother Joe showed up at my door and informed me she and the boys would be living with me until they found a place to live. Holy Crap ... I don't think so I told RC! He reiterated that it was not a suggestion, letting me know I didn't have a choice. Joe pushed me up against the wall, having a gun sticking down the front of his pants and said, "You will do this and be happy about it, do I make myself clear?" I was pregnant with my second son, working a good job, and seriously did not need this sort of headache from Dorothy, her kids, and especially treats from my father and Joe since I had made such an effort to stay clear of both, only seeing my mother when I knew RC was out of town or at work. I asked them both why she couldn't stay with them, as I had one small child and another on the way and only a one-bedroom apartment. My father did not hesitate a moment when he got in my face and told me "Because she is going to live here" after he again pushed me up against the wall so hard, I felt dizzy.

Dorothy openly admitted that she needed some distance to think things over and do what was best for her boys. They had never been so far away from her family and from Gary, and they apparently all missed him terribly even though they only got to see their husband and father on weekly visits in the prison yard, decided it was better than nothing. Gary wrote to Dorothy almost daily, begging her to return. One night as we sat on the back porch watching the kids play, I assured her Gary was being selfish and his only concern was for himself, not for her and their boys. I tried to make her understand that as time passed, it would get better once she found a job and a place to live, got the boys in school, etc. and it could not happen quick enough for me. Dorothy knew I did not want her and the boys there for many reasons that she already knew. I had distance myself from my father and brothers and she was aware of this, and I did not want a part of any of this. The other was simply we had way too many people jammed into a one-bedroom apartment. I told her RC and Joe had threatened me if I did not allow her to stay. She said she felt bad about it but was desperate and unsure of so many things in her own life. My feelings did not seem to faze her much; she had become so calloused to others and their feelings, just as Gary was ... she just didn't care apparently about anyone except Gary.

Dorothy's migraines got worse, and she felt she needed the support of her family to raise her sons, as they had always been close and helped her in almost daily care of them since Gary had been in and out of prison their entire lives. No matter the pressure from her family to divorce Gary, she could not do it. She ultimately returned to Arizona with her sons in tow and settled in Phoenix, and in all honesty, I could not have been happier for myself. Dorothy did not say anything to anyone, just left early one morning, and I got slapped around a bit as RC and Joe thought I'd run her off. Being well into my pregnancy, I felt they wouldn't beat on me too badly, just slapped around a bit until finally I told them at the top of my lungs that she was a crazy bitch and just like Gary, and I didn't need or want this or them in my life. They both called me a selfish bitch and left. I only ended up with some bruising on my face, one eye and chest and felt blessed they had not punched me in the stomach area to hurt my unborn child. I luckily did not see either of them for months, which was more than perfect for me. After that, I always managed to see my mother when I knew the two of them were not around.

Luckily for me, Raymond Smith, my then husband, who was a soldier in the US Army. We married, and he almost immediately got stationed in El Paso, Texas, to train with a Vulcan Chaparral unit that was going to be sent to Europe in eighteen months. I felt for the first time in my life I was going to be free of the Tisons, the criminal activity and the abuse. I was happy to go so far away. My mother was heart-broken because she felt she would not see the boys for years, but I knew I had to get away from this family once and for all. I could not pack up quickly enough.

What I realized during the time Dorothy and the boys stayed with me was that she was as corrupt as Gary and had developed an antagonism with the law as well. All those years of brainwashing and thinking of ways to get him out of prison had taken its toll on her, and she no longer thought like a normal person but rather like Gary, my other brothers, and RC.

After the escape and even still after all this time, I have often wondered how a mother – any mother – could put her own sons in the situation she put them in by planning this escape. Remember, she was not there at the prison in July 1978 .... she sent her sons with shotguns to assist Gary and Randy with their escape.

Donnie Joe, Ricky, and Ray grew up as what appeared to be polite, obedient, reserved, and quiet. Ricky and Ray spent most of their time with cousins from Dorothy's side of family but were always together. Donnie Joe, at a young age, had started out exploring options of education and his future and so became the brunt of many jokes by his brothers and cousins about his goals, as they were so different from all of theirs.

After Dorothy returned not only to Arizona but to those weekly prison visits, as mother had told me in letters, Gary had convinced her he had made a new friend inside who was the answer to his next escape. Bobby Tuzon was serving a sentence for second degree murder and was placed on kitchen duty with Gary; they also had cells next to one another. Bobby, according to all the transcripts I've read, was a model prisoner who just wanted to do his time and return to his family. Gary learned he was a pilot and immediately decided he could benefit him in his upcoming escape attempt. Gary, of course, went through all his details over a period, and Bobby informed him he wanted nothing to do with it, according to Bobby Tuzon's sworn documents after the fact. Gary continued to put pressure on him, even having his wife threatened by Dorothy who lived in the Phoenix area. This guy, according to transcripts, as well as his wife, were terrified and asked to speak with Warden Caldwell to expose Gary's plans. The warden took no pity on him, calling him someone with a vivid imagination and a flat-out liar. Bobby requested to be sent back to maximum security inside the walls to prevent any future contact with Gary. Warden denied his request, so Bobby ultimately planned his own escape by cutting through a fence and sitting outside the fence, waiting for the guards to arrest him, making no attempt to run. It was his way of getting back into maximum security and away from Gary. Unfortunately for him, Gary put the word through other prisoners' that he was as good as dead.

One of Joe's cronies, also a pilot, got arrested in Texas with a load of drugs during this same time frame. He used the only ace he had to plea bargain and that was Gary's planned escape for the late spring which Joe had told him about. Texas officials contacted the warden, but again he took no action. Of course, Bobby Tuzon heard of this through the prison grapevine and decided to go above the Warden's head to Ellis MacDougall, head of the Department of Corrections. Bobby told Ellis MacDougall that he had attempted and escape, cutting the hole through a fence and sat right outside waiting for guards to arrest him just so he could be placed back into maximum security and away from Gary. Ellis MacDougall believed him and had Gary immediately sent back to maximum security as well. However, within a short period of time, the Warden transferred

Gary back to minimum security where he and Randy Green-walt ultimately escaped with the help of his three sons on Sunday morning, July 28, 1978.

Bobby Tuzon filed a civil suit against the warden and State of Arizona and settled for $58,000 for the danger he was exposed to and no cooperation or safe keeping from the warden. He was paroled in 1985 and entered law school.

The State of Arizona also settled with other victims' families for $975,000. All this could have been prevented if prison officials would have listened, took caution, and kept Gary and Randy in maximum security. But for whatever reason ... they did not.

Chapter 5
My First Experience with Law Enforcement & Court; Oxnard, Calif.

Although mom had sat in front of judges before my first experience was at the ripe old age of ten in Oxnard, California, in early 1958. R.C. and brother Joe robbed a grocery store just a couple of miles around the corner from our rental house. I recalled them telling my mother they had gotten work but did not actually start until the following day so they would be right back when leaving early one morning.

Being the "intelligent men", they were (and I surely say this with tongue in cheek), they robbed a store right in *our* neighborhood with a .32 caliber pistol and in broad daylight, leaving their car parked in front of the store. I have always said, "Desperate people do desperate things" but this really took the cake. If they were going to rob a store, could they not have at least gone to a neighboring town ... but right in our own neighborhood where folks knew who they were. The clerk recognized them both, called police, and they quickly located R.C. and Joe at the house. Apparently one of the witnesses also recognized the car and the occupants and was able to tell them who they were and where we lived. It never took long for people in our neighborhoods to know who we – or at least my brothers. If R.C. and my brothers were not conducting criminal activity right away whenever we moved to a new place, they were surely screwing the neighbors' wives and daughters. They were not only criminals but predators as well.

Wherever we lived, mom had always taken in ironing for what I referred to as "rich folks" for extravagant things like food and clothes. We were doing someone's ironing when R.C. and Joe returned looking nervous and acting strange. R.C. told mom if anyone came looking for either one of them to just tell them they were not there. He told her to tell them they were both working at a cotton camp somewhere near Arvin. Mom never liked to lie but always did as R.C. told her. She insisted we go back to ironing and leave them alone in the bathroom of all places.

Before long, the police arrived and stated they were looking for R.C. and Joe Tison. Mom told them exactly what R.C. had told her but she never was particularly good at that lying thing. She knew it was wrong but obeyed. The officers insisted they come in and check. This was years before anyone ever thought of asking for a search warrant or such; it was just the way it was in those days. If the police thought they should come in and check, then of course mom allowed them to come in and check, knowing full well they were going to find them but never anticipated they had done anything too awfully wrong, as she always believed the best of them. She believed in R.C. like no other person ever had, she trusted him completely and, of course, Joe being the Golden Boy, never would have done any too awfully wrong in her opinion. After finding both R.C. and Joe hiding, they called for additional officers and started tearing our house apart. At that point, my only concern was about the ironing because we had worked hard at getting it done and they were throwing it around, searching for whatever, although I had told them it was someone else's clothes; they did not seem to care much. In my naive, ten-year-old mind I couldn't help but think, "This just isn't fair, and they should show us some respect. After all, it was us who had worked so hard, not those assholes hiding in the bathroom." Apparently, they didn't care much about what I thought and had ask me several times to be quiet.

Mom then quickly put my younger sister and Larry and I inside a closet, for safekeeping I assumed. I spent many years in therapy as an adult for claustrophobia for those little visits to the closet, which became frequent over the years whenever the police came to our house. She never gave thought to the long term, negative effects this would have on us; it was her simple-minded attempt to keep us safe from harassment of police officers, RC, and brothers. The officers immediately tore us from the closet and moved us back into the living room near the ironing board, pushing and shoving the entire way. They found almost $600 in the laundry hamper in the bathroom. At least now I knew what R.C. and Joe were doing in there together after returning home. I always knew they were strange ... but this was strange even for them.

The officers made Larry, my younger sister, and me stand next to the dining room table with our hands behind us. They then stripped searched my mother right in front of us. She was so humiliated and shamed for lying to them and then being put through this in front of her small children. They found $10 in her bra and laid it on the table along with the stolen money they had retrieved from the bathroom. I attempted to explained that we had earned this money, it was not stolen, but they insisted they had to take it as well, and again, told me to be quiet. They handcuffed my mother after *graciously* allowing her to redress and placed her in a police car. She was so humiliated having been stripped search down to her panties in front of her small children. She had always been shy and private about her body.

When none of the officers were looking, Larry picked up the $10 and put it in his pants pocket saying to me, "You and mom earned this!" Unfortunately, one of the officers saw him from the kitchen and not only took it but placed him in handcuffs as well. At this point I just started screaming, "Please don't take Larry and my mother, they didn't do anything wrong. We really did work for that $10." Little did I know at the time, brother Larry had long since been solicited into a life of crime by our father and older brothers. It was years later that I learned this about him and was devastated, as I thought he learned from example as us girls had, that crime didn't pay....I was wrong about him.

A sentence of five years to life was given R.C. by the judge in a California Correctional Facility with a strong lecture of how he had led his son into a life of crime and would also have to serve time, only in a different facility where R.C. could no longer corrupt him. For Gary and Joe, it was too late, they had already chosen his lifestyle. Joe returned many times to crime and always ended up back in prison for one thing or another, as did Larry. As it turned out, the use of the gun in the commission of a felony is what caused RC's prison sentence to be so lengthy. I was always intrigued and listened intensely to judges, even though they were sentencing family members ... they seemed so smart and knew just about everything about everything, or at least I thought so in my young mind.

My mother's sister, Aunt Ozella and Uncle Floyd, lived in Oxnard, just a short distance away and we all felt safe and secure around them, I wanted very badly to just live with them forever. Unfortunately, at least for me, this never happened. Until her death later in life, I remained close to her, even making trips to see her in Redding, Calif., where they retired, to visit her and Uncle Floyd, cousins, nieces, and nephews. She was always such an inspiration to me and showed unconditional love to us kids and to our mother.

Aunt Ozella never liked R.C.; she continued to tell mom he was a bad seed, and to just stay there and they would help us, but it was off to Casa Grande. I never did understand that since R.C. and Joe were obviously going to serve time in California, and we certainly knew that mother would sacrifice whatever to visit them both. mother had some preconceived notion that Gary would help her as he was not in prison at that time, after all, she was his mother, her husband had just been sentenced to five years to life in prison, and she had three little ones to care for.

The first night we returned from California was spent at Dorothy and Gary's house near Maricopa. We were hungry and tired from the trip, but Dorothy insisted she only had enough food for the next day and didn't want to make anything additional. I remember my mother crying before going to sleep and promised us she would find a place for us to live right away. I also remember how mean and cruel Gary was. He kept cussing and raving saying, "If the stupid SOBs were dumb enough to get caught, then they should do time, and now I've got extra mouths to feed with these ass-holes," not even referring to mother as his "Mom," but "ass-holes that showed up at the door without any notice and expected to stay there." I kept thinking my mother would realize what R.C. had put us through and would finally come to her senses and just not have any more con-tact with him. Boy, was I wrong!

The letters started coming, and of course mom shared most of them with us kids, like I really cared. R.C. and Joe both had "gotten religion" again and were going to live a wholesome Christian life when returning to society. Of course, mom believed every word of it because she had always been a God-fearing woman and wanted so badly to believe this could and would be true. She continued to carry the thought of us all getting up on Sunday morning, having breakfast, and off to church where R.C. and Joe would probably want to sit right on the front row, so they didn't miss anything. Somehow, even as a young girl, I knew this was never going to happen, but everyone needs a dream and that was mothers'.

Chapter 6
Prison Visits
with Our Father

I am not quite sure how she did it, but the following day we had a house to move into. I knew when we left Gary's she wasn't going back; I could see the hurt in her eyes and heard it in her voice. I knew she had hoped for just a bit of compassion from Gary considering her husband had just been sent to prison and she was alone with small kids, no money, and no hope. However, both she and us kids were unwanted in his house, were treated badly, and refused food after traveling all the way from California, and he and Dorothy both knew we were all hungry. As we all laid in one bed trying to sleep, I could hear mother softly praying for God's help and quietly sobbing.

The house was a small, one-bedroom house on French Street. Growing up on the south side of the tracks, I did not know we were so poor because everyone else in that neighborhood was in the same shape, this was no different. Our new landlady on French Street was a kind black woman named Mrs. White. I always thought that was rather strange, but as usual, I was always curious and wanted explanations for everything. She was so kind to my mother that I never pushed the name issue. She allowed us to move in without the first month's rent, had the swamp cooler serviced, and even put food in the kitchen for us. We thought we were living high, or at least I thought so as we put on a pot of beans and made some cornbread. Mother kept reminding us that God had shined on us with his glory, and we now had a place to live, food, and it was cool inside. At least, from my standpoint, we did not have to tolerate R.C., and that alone made it better than the past.

The first thing mother did was write R.C. in prison and tell him how well we were doing. She probably just forgot to tell him she walked miles each morning to pick cotton all day, then did ironing in the evenings for other people. She didn't drive the old 55' Buick we had because she simply couldn't afford the $1 worth of gas, we put in it each time we drove it, and told me how healthy she was getting by walking so much. Damn, you talk about a positive attitude. She knew all about drinking lots of water, probably because there was never enough food to go around and walking to stay healthy long before it became popular in the 1980s. I asked her once if she told R.C., and she informed me he had enough on his mind without worrying about us. Right! A thermostatically cooled prison cell, three square meals a day (and I'll bet it wasn't the shit food we were eating), and oh yeah, he had the nerve to write us kids and tell us he had a colored TV to watch, which surely didn't go over well with me considering we didn't have a TV at all. That really made my day! As if it couldn't get worse, she would send him money orders so he could buy candy and cigarettes in the prison store.

Things were getting better though. Mom got a job in a laundry house just across the ditch from where we lived. She worked for Mr. Forsythe in a hot laundry house behind where the Desert Sands Bar now sits on Pinal Avenue. I kept thinking "at least she didn't have to walk so far to pick cotton every day." She was able to take my younger sister and I with her to work when there was no school and I guess you might say that was my first job. I got to do the sheets and towels in an old wringer washer and had access to Coca-Cola and peanuts and got paid five cents per hour. It took a bit of work from my tired, poor mother, and she probably figured I could not screw up towels and sheets too much. As I look back, I realized Mr. Forsythe probably wasn't paying me but rather it was coming out of my mother's wages. She worked hard and needed the help, and I felt good about contributing something and helping my mom. We still did ironing at night, and the trick was to get it across the little irrigation ditch gate we had to cross without dropping them in the water. When you work this hard you find yourself being awfully careful. I was pretty much a clumsy, awkward kid so this was a real accomplish-ment for me.

I learned from some friends about welfare. Most of the folks in this neighborhood were getting it, and *we* could get money and food certificates, but mother would not hear of it. She came from a decent, hardworking farming family, the Dixons, and none of them ever took a handout. Even at the ripe old age of eleven, I explained to her none of the Dixons had their husbands in prison and young, hungry mouths to feed. I did not let it go. I researched this welfare thing and finally convinced mother to at least get commodities. Wow! Peanut butter, great cheese, and things we had not been able to afford before. I'll never forget the saddened, distressed look on this precious woman's face as we put $1 worth of gas and two quarts of oil in the old Buick and stood in line at the National Guard Armory in downtown Casa Grande with the rest of the poor folks. The line was long, and when I found an old rag on the ground, near where we were standing, and told Mom I would use it to go out and check the oil while we were waiting and prayed it had not all leaked out. A dollars' worth of gas and two quarts of oil was standard for the old Buck. I had never seen such defeat on her face before, standing in line to take handouts with the other poor folks. Many years later, she revealed to me that the only reason she agreed to do this was because I had asked so many people and researched this welfare thing and was only trying to make her life a bit easier. Being the honest woman she was, she told the caseworker about the ironing we did at night, and we lost some of the commodity benefits. She said honesty always paid off. I tried to rationalize all this as our goodies had been cut considerably. All we must do, she said, was to work a bit harder and longer each day, and we could make up the difference. Unfortunately, the more ironing we did, the more commodities we lost. This was not making much sense to this kid who had researched the welfare thing and thought I had figured it all out.

Friday was always payday and we always had tacos on payday. I was a skinny, ugly kid but could almost eat my weight in homemade tacos. Friday night, after mother, Larry and my younger sister and I sat down to eat, my brother, Gary stormed into the house. It was one of those rare occasions when he was not in prison for one thing or another. He just pushed me away from the table after only one taco and told me to go outside. He surely did not have to tell me twice, as he scared the hell out of me, even as a young girl. If I had not left, he inevitably would have kicked me away from the table with his steel pointed cowboy boots. I do not think I ever saw him without them. He also always wore western shirts, dressing completely like a cowboy, however, I doubt he was ever on a horse and truly did not have the morals of any cowboy I had ever know. Cowboys are honorable, generally kind, and generous ... Gary was none of these.

Years later, my mother had told me Gary still wore cowboy boots, even in prison. As sad as it was, according to mother, it was his trademark. She said he had weak ankles and they allowed his boots for medical purposes, for additional support. He had convinced the warden they were for support due to his back problem and weak ankles. Anyone who ever wore cowboy boots would know they offered little to no support and were often more uncomfortable than ordinary shoes. Gary was a calculated manipulator and generally told people what they wanted to hear to get his way about any and everything. He was also known to carry a small pistol inside his boot, even while in prison.

His deep-set eyes were plain scary; it set him apart from other normal human beings I had ever known and never showed any sort of emotion, good or bad. They were basically expressionless. Being two different colors also added to the mix of scary for me, as one was sort of an amber color and the other hazel. I only saw this briefly from time to time, as I never looked at him for long, as his response would be something to the effect of "what the hell are looking at you stupid bitch."

I didn't know the word "sociopath" as a child; however, I knew Gary was a cold, calculating person who had no remorse for his actions. He was cruel and had no compassion for anyone. Considering his actions in retrospect, I was right on. Guess you might say it was my first psychological evaluation of another person. Knowing now what I did not know then was he was a classic textbook example of a sociopath with psychotic tendencies, making him an extremely dangerous human being, which was later confirmed. I used him to write a thesis in college, but of course, using a fictitious name.

At that point, I decided to get an education, make lots of money, take care of my younger sister and mother, and have tacos any night of the week I wanted, and Gary was never going to be welcomed in my home! I am 72 years old and there has never been a time when making tacos that I don't refer to it as "payday." Some things just stay with you.

***

I was devastated after three months to learn my mother had been putting money aside for a visit to see R.C. Each night after us kids went to bed; she would iron an extra dozen or so clothes for traveling money. At that time, people paid by the dozen, whether it was tablecloths or shirts or dresses. I ask – no, I begged – to stay with Mrs. Leonard, but mom wouldn't hear of it. "He is your father, and you should be happy to go see him," she would say. After all, he had given his life to the Lord, and it was all going to be different when he got out. Right! I never did buy into any of that. R.C. had always told mother what she wanted to hear, and I already knew this wasn't going to be the exception.

Mother informed us we were going to see our father the following week, I knew this was going to take more than $1 worth of gas, which was what we normally put in the old Buick when going to church. I must have asked a million questions like which hotel are we going to stay in and can we eat in restaurants. Little did I know at the time, there were no restaurants, no hotels, and no luxuries, only baloney and Spam sandwiches on the side of the road. No cheese, lettuce, and tomatoes with your favorite chips...just baloney and bread. To this day, I simply cannot stand the smell of baloney, which is one of my families' favorites, and I still feel a sealed can of Spam can contaminate my entire pantry of other foods and refuse to have it in my home.

Mother packed boxes with blankets and put them on the back seat floorboard even with the seat to make a bed for us. This wasn't exactly the hotel I had envisioned. We would leave after sundown, so it was not so hot. The temperature would drop from 115 degrees all the way down to 102. The old Buick did not have air conditioning, and she was convinced by R.C. that even if it did the car would use too much gas by turning it on. This was coming from a man who had the nerve to write this after telling us he had steak for dinner while sitting in his air-conditioned cell watching color TV. He never ceased to amaze me! We would usually get on the west side of Yuma before she would get too tired to drive; after all, she had worked all day before starting out on this journey.

My late husband Frank and I had a boat in San Diego Harbor in the 1990s, so we frequently traveled this same road. It is now Interstate 8; the old highway runs parallel to the freeway, and I could see those big old cottonwood and tamarack trees beside the road where we would stop, eat, and sleep on those visits to see RC. After numerous trips, mother had it down to a science. She would whip out the baloney or Spam and bread, and we would sit by the side of the road. Once she had bought cookies *and* cheese *and* soda pop. She must have ironed another extra dozen clothes for all these goodies. I really thought we were living rather high on the hog. But my curious nature always wondered what our dear father had for dinner, being angry in my thoughts of him and the hardship he had placed onto my mother and us kids. After a while, I began to realize how much pain this caused mother when I brought things like this up, so I worked at keeping my thoughts to myself. She would always remind me when I did bring it up that R.C. had given his life to the Lord and was a changed man. That always brought a smile to my face but for a different reason than mother thought – I knew he was blowing smoke and my mother bought into every word.

After we ate, she would always instruct us to get some sleep. My younger sister and I slept on the makeshift bed leveled with boxes in the backseat while Mom slept on the front seat. Larry had decided to lift the trunk and sleep there. Little did I know at the time he was robbing and stealing from other poor folks who were sleeping on the side of the road alongside of us. This, of course, is why he choose to sleep in the trunk and mother would not hear him get out of the car at night. I never could figure out why he always had money for the candy machines in the visiting room at the prison while we were visiting R.C. However, one night I got out of the car to pee, and I saw him throwing a purse away after taking the money out of it. I knew even then that it took the lowest of the lowest person to steal from poor people sleeping on the side of the road with their children. My whole opinion of Larry changed from that point on. I had always loved him so much and thought he was different from RC, Joe, and Gary...he wasn't. If there was any justification to this, at least R.C. and Joe operated from the Robin Hood theory, robbing from the rich to give to the poor...meaning themselves. Stealing from the poor folks with children on the side of the road was exceptionally bad.

After seeing Larry do this, our relationship was never the same. I attempted to distance myself from him even while living in a small, one bedroom house with mother and my younger sister. At this point in life, I took up reading. It was a form of escape from reality.

This was the first of many trips to visit RC in prison, and then of course, extending the trip up to see Joe in Lompoc Prison, each one worse than the one before. My heart would break to see my mother work so hard, dragging her young children across the desert into California in a hot car, sleeping on the side of the road and eating crappy food for a man who was so ungrateful and unappreciative in every way. Mother always insisted we pray together before eating. I had always believed in God and had strong faith; however, it was an effort on my part to be grateful for what we were eating, and on the side of the road no less.

Even after all these years, while watching movies I realize just how many prisons we had visited R.C. in. It troubles my soul, even though I love my mother dearly, that she drug us small kids into these horrible places such as San Luis Obispo Men's Colony, Victorville, San Quentin, Lompoc, and others as R.C. was transferred from one to the other; I never knew why, but he was.

San Quentin was the worst trip for all of us, especially for my mother since it was located so much further up the California Coast. I had nightmares for years about the draw bridges going into and around San Quentin Prison. Our car was old, and I always prayed the brakes would work as it was like we were going to fall off the bridges. I could always tell mother was scared to death and that caused even more fear for a young girl who did not want to be there anyway.

Chapter 7
Continued Prison Visits and R.C.'s Release from Prison

As the prison visits with mother to see RC continued for many years, either mother really felt she needed to see him or she thought she was doing the right thing by taking her children to this awful place to visit their father who, at least I, could have certainly done without. RC and I never got along, as far back as I can remember. I used to wonder why he hated me so much, as I was treated differently than the others. I finally concluded later in life that he knew I had him figured out, he knew I knew he was a deceitful evil man, and I believed his long-term goal was to keep me in fear and intimidation of him to keep me quiet ... sometimes it worked, mostly not.

Even though we were so damn poor, and mother had to work so hard I still felt life was better because we didn't have to tolerate R.C., except for the visits. We did not have to tolerate his inappropriate touching, beatings, and constant belittling of our character. However even as a young girl, while in the visiting rooms, we would have to endure other old men looking at us as if they would eat us alive if given the opportunity, it completely creped me out. I do not ever remember using the bathroom in one of those visiting rooms out of shear fear one of those old men would follow me in there. I learned at an early age not to drink much water and be able to hold it till we got out of that place. One time I thought I was going to burst, and as soon as we entered the parking lot, I ran to a tree and peed behind it. Mother gave me quite an ass whipping for doing this, but it was still better than going into the public restrooms in the visiting room at the prison.

RC finally got released on parole after a few years, and mother just knew things were going to be better. R.C. was going to take care of her and us kids and attend church with us. The first thing he said when returning home was, "We have to move out of this damn dump, and I ain't renting from no nigger woman." We had fixed it up and cleaned it up well and did not refer to it as "a dump"; it had been home all the time he was in prison, watching his colored TV in an air-conditioned cell and eating steak and other quality foods, not living in poverty as we did. After all, we would not have been living there at all if he had not robbed the grocery store and went to prison for years. Also, Mrs. White had been so kind to us all these years and had helped my mother considerably. We considered her our friend. She had even taken me to church with her on occasions. If you have never attended a Black Spiritual Church, then you simply haven't lived. These new friends of mine knew how to sing and worship. We were Pentecostal, and I just thought the church we attended got it on with spiritual dancing, etc., we were considered Holy Rollers by the public. Those were some of my favorite times with Mrs. White because I always loved to sing and praise. Mother always had told me it was the highest form of worship to

God, and it was always more enjoyable to me than the preaching or prayer request.

In the old Pentecostal Churches we attended, you always could predict what prayer request were going to be given by each person. My friend Sissy and I used to whisper to each other when specific women would stand to request prayer from the other congregates. One elderly lady always would ask that they pray for her husband who drank booze and was a philanderer of women of the night. Being so young, of course, we always thought they were too old to do it and could not imagine her husband chasing any women, especially women of the night. A few others seem to utilize it as a gossip session to let others know "So and so's husband or son or daughter needed special prayer due to etc., etc." I always felt it was a way to spread gossip and doing it in the form of a prayer request. Even as a young girl, it disturbed me that people would say such things in church as mother was death on gossiping and simply did not allow it, always telling us if someone we knew needed prayer, go to God quietly and ask him to help them, bless them or meet their needs, whatever the situation was, but never gossip.

At that time, Pentecostals were not allowed anything like cosmetic makeup, piercing of ears, cutting of hair, dancing, going to movie theaters, public swimming pools, listen to rock'n'roll music, or wearing anything that might be considered revealing. Men's pants or jeans were out of the question for women and were looked down upon by the church, even if you worked in the fields. No exceptions whatsoever. These strict rules imposed by the church ensured most young members were isolated and joked about in schools and in public. They referred to us as "Holy Rollers," and we were the constant blunt of cruel and hurtful remarks.

But Mrs. White's church just sang and praised the Lord, using washboards, spoons, tambourines, and piano for music, clapping their hands all the time. I always felt like I had been washed clean of any sins when leaving their church situated just west of North French Street. Not that a girl of my age would have had any sins to be washed away, but the fiery walls of hell had been so imbedded in us by our church leaders always made us feel the need to be washed free of our sins, no matter how small they might have been.

R.C. got a job as a foreman for Hoyt Farms on Selma Highway. With this job came a big old house that needed some serious cleaning and repairs. As mom and us girls had done so many times before, we cleaned and painted, putting those old curtains up to give it that "homey" look, as mom referred to it. I was always amazed at how she made the same curtains look like they fit in so many different houses and they always looked good after we starched and ironed them. As we worked for weeks getting this place livable, I kept thinking the place on French Street was much better, although it was smaller; we had already done all this stuff to make it nice. But R.C. said in no uncertain terms, "This is where we live; if you don't like it, move out." When he said things like this, I always wondered where is a young girl supposed to go when her father would say this to her? Oh well, it could and had been worse. It was one of those deal-with-it situations.

He explained to mom that he just did not have time to

attend church with her, but he assured her he was praying all the time while he was working. This did not come as any surprise to me since I had always known he was blowing smoke in all those letters that came from prison. And I am sure he was not praying when he was out drinking and chasing whores, or conjuring up some get rich scheme, but mom was just sure his heart was right with God. And of course, as leaving he'd always ask her to pray for him while he was out there working hard and making us a living.

Of course, as always, that farm job did not last long, and we moved onto Center Street, I always liked being able to go to the drug store on Florence Street for a cherry Coke with my housecleaning and babysitting money that nobody knew I had, making my visit last as long as possible so I could just sit and watch people. Nobody ever yelled at me in there or told me to get out. I could just sit there for the longest time. When I did not have money for a cherry Coke, I would ride my bike around town. Mr. Serrano from Serrano's Western Wear used to see me and always offered me one of those small bottles of Coca-Cola. I remember thinking he had to be the richest and nicest guy in the whole town. After all, he just gave people bottles of Coca-Cola. Once I got older, I realize he probably just felt sorry for me, knowing what our family life was like, as most of the locals knew. We had no family secrets; most everything my father and brothers did were on the front page of the newspapers or on the 6 o'clock news. My brothers were always in trouble with the law. I am sure everyone in town knew all about my family. I was just a young, curious girl who liked people and rode my bike around town visiting, always going by the Pentecostal church we attended at Fifth and

Lincoln because there was always someone there or something going on. If you showed up, the ladies of the church would inevitably give you a job of some sort, which I never really minded. It was part of that old Pentecostal way of thinking of "working your way to heaven" that was so strongly instilled in my young mind.

On Thursdays, the ladies group made fried pies. It was labor intensive, and they all worked so hard starting the night before preparing the different types of fruits to be placed into them at their individual homes, then of course, bringing them all together in the kitchen part of the church. Starting early Thursday morning, they made dough, rolled, and cut with saucers and meticulously sealed them around the edges before placing them in large skillets of hot oil. They laid them on a table to drain and when cooled, we would all help them packaged into individual bags, labeled, and stapled. I rounded up an old wagon from somewhere and hauled those pies all over Casa Grande, selling each one I had taken with me. I was always careful about change and getting all the money back to the lady's group because they helped others with these funds i.e., Missionaries, Christmas candy for children, Boys Ranch, etc. I do not ever remember my mother missing an opportunity to work for the church and raise funds either through Fried Pies or Quilting Quilts that were sold. I once asked her why she worked so hard and she said with tears in her eyes, "It's too late for my boys, but perhaps I can make a difference in another's life." Wow, that was heavy for me to comprehend at the time but later figured it out. She always said, "you give from the heart, whether it be your time or money and what they do with it after that is between them and God." I still practice that with homeless people or others who cross my path, not being judgmental, just giving from the heart.

Several folks would give me a tip or a bottle of Coke while I was pulling my wagon around town selling Pies, which made me extremely happy and worth all my efforts. Because I had spent so much time riding my bike around town and knew so many folks, they freely bought the pies from me. The fact that they were wonderful made it easier for me but again, I think a lot of people bought from me just because they felt sorry for me. So often folks would say "just two please" and then say, "oh what the heck, let me have six." I thought at one point I was the world's greatest sales-person but also recognized the damn pies were wonderful.

Unfortunately, it took me 50 years to obtain the original dough recipe from one of my older cousins, Naomi, who was the only one who knew it and it had never been written down, it was all in her head. With my older sister, Martha and two other cousins from California, Theresa Nichols, and Ricki Sue Gustafson went to visit her one Sunday afternoon and as she gave us the recipe, Therese wrote it all down and we went back to my ranch and spent all afternoon making Fried Pies. We ate them till we were sick but laughed and had such a good time knowing we had finally acquired the infamous Fried Pie Recipe (which I have included in this book).

When I was the ripe old age of 13, Arizona Public Service had signs around town offering a free cooking class at its office. I could not wait to get home to ask mother if I could go. I had memorized the poster and was giving her all the details when Joe came into the kitchen and told mother she should let me go to it. He laughed a deep laugh, saying,

"Look at her, she's ugly, got buck teeth, stringy hair, skinny as a rail and no tits. We've got to let her learn how to cook or nobody will ever marry her, and we'll have to support her the rest of her life." I remember going into the backyard, under the clothesline and crying for hours as I had never thought of myself as all those negative qualities. Whatever happened to building self-esteem in children? I had seen families on television and knew this was wrong. But with Joe, being the Golden Boy that he was with my parents, mother just smiled and said, "Joe that wasn't very nice." Was not nice, hell! I spent many years reliving that little episode and honestly believing I was ugly, and nobody ever would want me unless I was a terrific cook.

One day, I was watching the girls track team run the track from the bleachers at the junior high school, I decided to run behind them. The coach quickly notice that I was faster than anyone and could have passed them all but knew "my place," and I was not a part of the team. He walked toward me afterwards, and I thought I was going to get a lecture, but instead he asked me where I learned to run like that. I was too embarrassed to tell him it was part of my survival of having to outrun my father. RC was quick-tempered, and if I could outrun him, he would not beat me nearly as bad once he had me within his clutches, after he'd had a little time to simmer down, as mother would say.

This coach asked me if I wanted to be a part of the track team, and I had to tell him I could not afford the shorts or shoes and my mother's Pentecostal religion prohibited me from wearing shorts. He took a deep breath, as to take it all in, then told me the team had a small fund for such things. He asked me my shoe size and the next day brought me a pair of beautiful tennis shoes into the cafeteria when I was working along with some brand-new socks and a pair of white shorts. Damn, I thought I had died and gone to heaven. He gave me a printout of the schedule, and I was overwhelmed that I was a part of something so exciting. However, I did tell him I would not be able to attend out of town competitions, only the ones at the school. I believe from his look, he realized what my situation was and did not push it. At first, the other girls were not receptive to me, and I was shunned, but Lord have mercy when we won our first track meet, they were happy to have me as part of the team. I had never been a part of anything, especially a school team, and I was elated, not even being able to sleep that night due to the excitement.

Over the years, I volunteered as an advocate for abused children for more than twenty years, and numerous organizations that help young people. I even started an equine therapy business known as the W6Ranch Counseling Service to assist abused children in finding their way after living with an abusive parent or someone else in their lives. I've never given a child/youth a toy or clothing that I don't remember my excitement that day in the cafeteria when the Coach gave me those shoes, socks, and shorts for the Track Team, I always wanted to share that feeling with other unfortunate children/youth. It brought me such joy.

Now I had to decide how I was going to pull this off without my family knowing. I had to have a bike that I could ride to school instead of the school bus. We had a broken-down old bike at some point, but it just disappeared, never sure what happened to it. I had thought of a plan to wash my shorts and socks out before leaving for school and put them on the handlebars to dry. Once dried, I folded them nicely and put them in a book, and by track time, the shorts looked like they had been ironed. I started checking alleys and dumpsters for bits and pieces of bikes and finally had enough to put one together. Problem was .... I needed tires and rims. I went to a bike shop and asked the owner if I could possibly work off two tires. He seemed to like me and probably felt sorry for me, so he gave me a job sweeping out his shop after school. I worked so hard for him, doing lots of things around the shop, and it did not go unnoticed. After a week, not only did he give me two new tires and rims, but he also paid me. I thought he must be the most generous person in the world.

I would lie in bed at night thinking, "My plan is going to work," and it did. It was the first time in my life that I realized I could do something good and creative and get myself out of the horrible situation I lived in, if only for a few hours each day. Of course, I had to make up excuses to RC for not being in the fields earlier and for working after school. So, I could be at practice or meets, I had to lie, telling him I was in after school detention. Before he beat the crap out of me for not being able to work in the fields after school, he said "I don't even care what for." He just beat my ass. I sucked it up and determined to continue running track with the team, as I loved it.

When things got bad at home, I would go to Elliott Park and swing and think about what I was going to do with my life once I got an education. When not at Elliott Park I would go to BeDillon's Cactus Garden north of Florence Boulevard. There was a small box for donations, the honor system, I never went in unless I had a penny, nickel, or dime

to put into the box. I took the "Honor System" sign genuinely serious. BeDillion's Cactus Garden is now a restaurant
and I never go in for lunch or dinner that I don't look out
into the garden and remember that this was my place of
solace growing up, I spent many, many days just sitting in
the garden amongst the Cactus trying to figure it all out. I
once shared my story with the owner, and he hugged me
for the longest time, then smiled and said, "It cost a hell of
a lot more than a penny, nickel or dime now" meaning
dinner and drinks. We both laughed.

My dream and my goal seemed to carry me through
some tough years as the Cops continued to come to our
house, and the abuse continued ... but I had a plan, and nothing was going to get in my way.

I didn't much care anymore about what happened at
home. I tried to busy myself with school, babysitting, and
my friend, Sissy. Sissy lived in a big old house right across
the street from the Casa Grande Women's Club, just around
the corner from us. She was as ugly as I was; we must have
looked pathetic when walking around town together. I was
short and very skinny with long stringy hair, spaced, buck
teeth, and always looked like I was wearing somebody
else's clothes, but then, I was wearing hand-me-downs. Her
hair was long, very curly, and looked as though it had never
seen a brushing, but the real treat was her teeth; they
extended further out than her upper lip, and they were
extremely discolored. I remember asking her once and she
explained that she had a gum disease and couldn't brush
her teeth like normal people. That explained why there
were green. Hell, we were friends; I just accepted that and
never ask again. Besides that, she was the best jack's player

I ever played with and that was the game of my life, besides baseball and running track, and I was rather good at that too. I never remember a family member coming to one of my games or track meets. I always saw parents, grandparents, aunts, and uncles come watch the other girls. I never really thought too much about it until later in life.

Many years later, I saw Sissy at a funeral, and her hair was beautiful, her teeth had been fixed, and she was a rather attractive lady, although it broke my heart because she didn't remember me from childhood. I had kept a picture of the two of us for years that Mom Leonard had taken one day after a church lunch, one of the few pictures I had of my childhood. Sissy was a fond childhood memory.

The upper-class ladies of our small town played bridge once a week at the Casa Grande Women's Club. Sissy and I would sit under a big, old tree and watch all the "rich" ladies (as I referred to them then) drive up in their beautiful clean cars. I always thought rich people just had clean cars; later in life did I learn that they probably had them washed before going to the Women's Club. I told her each time we did this that when I grew up, I was going to have a beautiful, clean car and was going to go to the Women's Club. I'll never forget my first experience there as an adult, I had been invited as a potential member of Zonta International by Dr. Denton. I had a beautiful Lincoln, and it was shiny as a new penny, however when I went to leave the battery was low and Frank suggested I take his truck. I looked at him and said, "I've waited all my life to drive an expensive, beautiful car to the Women's Club." He didn't quite understand where I was coming from but knew it was important and took his battery out of his truck and installed it into my

Lincoln. I later told him the story of Sissy and I watching all the ladies come to the Women's Club in their beautiful, shiny cars. He hugged me for a long time, understanding why it was so important to me to drive my Lincoln, and whispered in my ear "Well we got you there Ms. Lynda and in your shiny, beautiful, clean car." As silly as it may sound, that was always one of my dreams, and it finally happened. It was one of those times I felt I had accomplished yet another of my childhood dreams." I was terribly sorry that Sissy wasn't sitting under the big old tree across the street to see me. I looked in that direction, as I got out of my car and smiled as I remembered those childhood dreams, we shared.

I eventually was honored to become a Court Appointed Special Advocate (CASA) for abused and neglected children in Pinal County. I took this very seriously, realize the importance of a child or children in an abusive situation and their need for an advocate, someone who would care enough to volunteer their time to make a difference in the lives. I would have died to have someone looking out for my best interest growing up, or even someone who just cared enough to protect me from both the physical, verbal, and sexual abuse that I experienced on a regular basis. After being trained and certified as a CASA by the Arizona Supreme Court, I attended a reception in the lobby of the courthouse. That was the first time I had ever been in a courthouse where one of my brothers or fathers weren't on trial for something or another. I was so proud, as I had worked hard making a good living, raising three beautiful children, active in volunteer work, active in the community and had built an impeccable reputation for myself. As I was standing with a group, I heard a man nearby in another group talking louder than necessary, making sure I heard, saying "CASA must be hard up for volunteers, I understand they now have a Tison volunteering," while looking directly at me. Everyone within earshot turned to look at me with blank looks as some of them apparently didn't know I was related to the Tisons. I sat down my glass of punch and quickly left, crying all the way home, realizing this is never, ever going to end no matter what I do with my life, apparently it always going to surface when you least expect it. I didn't feel I deserved this after working hard so many years in so many areas ... but here it was!

As it turned out, the man who made those ugly comments at the reception for CASAs was Pinal County Manager Stan Griffis. He was arrested and prosecuted in 2007 for six felony counts of fraud and liability. He ultimately pleaded guilty and had to pay $640,000 in restitution to our county. Rick Romley stated on the news "this is a true violation of public trust as Griffis used the money he stole from our county to pay off his cars, remodel his home, buy weapons, and put more than $100,000 in a family trust." However, this is the man who made such a detrimental comment for all to hear at a reception about my being a Tison and becoming an advocate. Little did he know, I became an advocate due to being raised by the Tisons and experienced every type of abuse possible and decided to spent time and effort to attempt to make sure it didn't happen to another child assigned to me.

I thought about it for months, finally deciding to write him a letter in prison, reminding him of the nasty comment he made about me at the reception in 2006. Of course, he didn't respond, but it gave me some peace in my heart to write the letter. Afterall, I wasn't the bad guy .... he was! And now he was in prison for an awfully long time.

These were the times and situations when I was reminded that I should have left this area, relocating anywhere but here, this was one of those times. Many people have asked me over the years why I didn't leave Pinal County, even Arizona. I seriously considered it, however I had three children and felt they would tell someone, perhaps a friend in secret, and someone would tell someone else, and I would eventually have to deal with it all over again. At least here, many folks knew me to be of good character and felt at some point it was better to deal with the consequences of their actions here, rather than start over someplace new. After the prison escape in 1978 I wished many times that I had left and moved anywhere, anywhere except here. We paid such a terrible price for their actions.

During the time we lived on Center Street, I tried to keep distance between R.C and myself, rarely being around the house. Although it wasn't hard to figure out there was a lot of criminal activity going on in this place. Larry and Joe both lived there, although Joe was married, or at least I think he was. I used to lie about whom I was related to so people wouldn't think I was bad too. Apparently, they all knew in school because I had very few, to no friends. I spent my time studying and learning and never got involved in anything except for running track and playing some baseball in junior high school.

I always sat in the rear of the classrooms hoping nobody would notice I was there. One day I was walking home from school feeling good about my grades, when I turned off

Florence Boulevard onto Center Street, I saw numerous police cars sitting around the house. Shit! What now?

Gary had escaped from prison again, and they were tearing our house apart looking for whatever. I just couldn't believe this was happening again. I had been saving baby-sitting money, and it was under my mattress in the bedroom that several of us shared. I just knew they were going to take the money because with my brothers, they would automatically assume it was stolen if it was hidden. Unfortunately, if it hadn't been hidden, my brothers would have stolen it from me. After the police finished, I sat on the back steps and couldn't help but wonder if the police had taken my money or had Joe or Larry found it before the police even got there.

So, did they take the money? I guess I'll never know.

Pentecostal Ladies Association (PLA)
Famous Fried Pies
Filling choices: Peach, Cherry, Apple, Pineapple, Apricot

Smash fruit and heat in pan on stove
Mix flour, sugar and a little salt and use to thicken fruit
    sauce.

Pastry:
5 cups Gold Medal Flour
2 tsp. baking powder
1 tsp. salt
¼ cup sugar
1 cup butter flavored Crisco
2 cups cream (carnation milk)

2 eggs

Put dry ingredients in a plastic bag and mix.
Put dry ingredients in bowl and add wet ingredients
And mix with hands.
Roll dough out till it is thin
Use saucer to cut dough in circle
Flip in hands like pizza dough
Lay flat and place filling inside
Dip finger in water and run around outside of pastry
Fold in half and seal with fork.
Heat Crisco in pan to deep fry the pies, drop them in until
    brown
Drain on paper towel and let cool.

Yields 50 Pies

Chapter 8
Leaving Casa Grande
and Attending High School
in Corcoran, Calif.

Again, one of my brothers was all over the news, and I was simply too embarrassed to go back to school. I was determined to get an education but seriously considered quitting after Gary escaped. He shot a prison guard, held a local woman and her child hostage, and then took her vehicle and was finally captured in a shootout on Lehmberg Street. Everyone in town, every channel on the news, and the local paper were talking about it, and I just didn't think I could face the disgrace once again in my early years of high school. I stayed in the backyard for days, only going in to eat and use the bathroom, thinking about what I could do, how I could handle the shame all the while, police were still coming around the house, asking questions and talking to every family member, neighbors and whomever else. I remember one police officer came into the backyard and asked me what I was doing, as I looked up at him with swollen eyes from crying, sitting on an old broken-down couch. I looked at him and said, "I'm trying to figure out a way to disappear from the face of this earth because I am so ashamed of what my family has done." He was kind, putting his hand on my shoulder assured me none of this was my fault. I asked him if he would mind telling everyone in high school and the rest of the world that. He just smiled and assured me everything would be all right, to just stay strong and positive.

My mother put me on a Greyhound bus and sent me to live with one of my older sisters and her husband in Corcoran, Calif. Nobody there knew of our family, and I could go to school like any other young girl.

It wasn't long before R.C. moved mother and my younger sister there as well. All I could think of is "here we go again." He worked on a farm about twelve miles south of town and three-quarters of a mile off the main highway. I was told I could no longer live with my sister but had to move home with them and work on the farm. Once again it was a dirty old farmhouse that had to be cleaned and fixed up. It wasn't long before Joe and Larry showed up, and I yet again wondered what kind of mess they would create here for us to have to live with here. Mom and I did a fairly good job of getting the old house in order when R.C. came in and announced I was going to chop cotton for him. I was always afraid to be around him if mom wasn't in the room because of his sexual appetite. He never actually penetrated me but liked to touch and rub up against me. Sometimes he would throw the newspaper all over the floor and then make me bend over to pick it up. I could always hear his loud, heavy breathing in the background, knowing he was probably masturbating, and it would make me physically sick. Of course, this only took place when mom wasn't around. I once tried to tell her, and she slapped me across the face, telling me my imagination was running away with itself. R.C. was a sociopathic bastard of a person who could easily convince you he was normal, friendly, and warm. I always loved having people around because he was on his best behavior, and nobody would have ever believed what he was really like. He only showed himself to those he didn't care about or respect ......like some of us kids. I knew that he was aware of the sexual behaviors of our brothers because once I heard them laughing about relatives not being as good as the girl down the road.

I walked the three-quarters of a mile to the road each day to catch the school bus. Sometimes I think R.C. would just hang out until I started down the road to catch the school bus. He traveled down the dirt road fast so he would throw dust all over me and yell out the window, "What the hell you going to school for? You think you're going to grow up to be the President of the United States, you fucking bitch? You should be out there working in the fields helping support this family, you worthless little bitch." I would just keep walking. I finally started carrying a wet cloth so I could get the dust off myself before getting on the bus. He told me at dinner one night that instead of coming home first I could just lay my books under the tree at the road and go directly into the cotton field. He convinced mom that I wouldn't have to walk so far if I did that and assured her, he would give me a ride to get my books and drive me home when I finished. He never did that either. I knew he was lying when he told her, and he winked at me as to keep my mouth shut. At first, I would wonder what he was doing getting out of his truck near the tree where my books were stored. I could see him from the field. Numerous times he took my homework assignments and destroyed them so I started memorizing them so I could get them done before going back to school the next day. I also got a job as a carhop at the A&W Root Beer stand on Friday and Saturday nights. Mom had promised me I could keep the money I made there for some clothes for school, as we never got paid to work for RC in the fields. He called it "paying our own way."

The Pentecostal Church my mom attended in Corcoran had a youth service on Friday nights. I always enjoyed attending before going to work but had to sit in the back since A&W required, we wear black pants, and the church didn't allow women wearing men's clothing. I considered myself a good Christian girl and enjoyed worshipping. I also used a bit of lip-gloss that my older sister had given me because my lips were always cracked from working in the fields. No color, just lip-gloss since coloring the lips was also a sin in this religion. There was a Sister Richardson that taught this youth service, and she had a daughter, Viola, who was a year older than I was. In the Pentecostal churches, they always call each other Brother and Sister Whatever. I had heard rumors about Sister Richardson's daughter, Viola and her activities in the country with numerous guys at a time. I tried telling my mother once about what I had heard, and she told me it was none of our business and that we shouldn't repeat it; she was always death on gossip. I never did again, but I would always worry about Viola for fear she would get hurt and didn't like the idea that guys laughed and made fun of her at school. She wasn't a friend because I knew she was a bad girl, and I didn't want anything to do with her, but I still worried about her.

One night while attending Youth Service before going to my job at A&W Root Beer stand, this Sister Richardson who ran the youth group, pointed her finger directly at me in the rear pew and said, "And all you little hussies that wear men's pants and color your lips are going to go straight to hell if you don't stop right now." I didn't consider myself a hussy, I was a good girl and good student, and knew in my heart that I was a good person. That accusation changed my life forever, as after a few seconds of thought, watching all the other kids turning around laughing at me, I stood up and informed her "I'll damn sure hold the door to hell open for her and her whore daughter," walked out and never went back to the Pentecostal Church. I heard everyone laughing because of what I had said as I practically ran out of the church. When I got home after work that night about midnight, I woke my mom up and told her what happened. She made excuses for Sister Richardson, and I explained to her that she could make me go to church but couldn't make me open my mind to what was being said. I suppose that was my first experience with a hypocrite since everyone knew what her daughter was doing and she made me feel like the scum of the earth about the pants I wore for work and trying to keep my lips from bleeding from working out in the fields, as they were constantly cracked. I never went back. I secretly always wished I could have been present when she met her judgment day before God.

As the farm hired more people to work in the fields, I knew R.C. couldn't bother me much. Between school and work, I was able to keep a good distance from him. I really liked the A&W job because all the "really cool" kids from school came there. They never had much to do with me other than ordering because I was still skinny, ugly and couldn't wear makeup, cut my own hair, or do any of the other things that girls did to make themselves look nice. All these things were against my mother's religion. Corcoran was a small town, and A&W was the only drive-in food place there at the time. One Friday night, I walked up to a red GTO with the best-looking guy I had ever seen. His name was Danny Griffith. He was nice to me, and I was so nervous I could hardly take his order. I had a mixture of relief and sadness when he left. He returned there every night that I worked. Finally, one night he asks me if I wanted to go cruising with him after I finished work. I was so thrilled I didn't want the night to ever end. We rode around for a while, and he finally took me back to my old Ford that I had bought for $200 to drive to work and school. We did this often, and finally one night he kissed me. I thought I was going to die. I finally had a boyfriend, or so I thought and felt life just couldn't get any better until he showed up the following weekend with a cute cheerleader. He came back after work alone and told me he took her out as a favor to a friend. Right! I couldn't go out on a date since R.C. didn't allow it. I just continued to see him after work and would sneak into the house so mom wouldn't know what time I got home. She knew I only worked until eleven I but once told her I had lots of cleaning to do after we closed. I would have done anything to continue seeing this gorgeous guy.

As the weekend cruising continued, we had what I thought was a relationship. He convinced me that all the girls in school "did it," and if I wanted to be cool I should too. He was going to show me how and promised it wouldn't hurt. It did hurt, and I didn't want to see him for a long time after that. I thought if this is what all the other girls do, then they could have it because I was embarrassed, and it hurt too much. As time passed and he kept coming in and apologizing, I started cruising with him again, and the relationship continued. Three months later, I realized I was pregnant. I had read some teen magazines that I kept hidden under my mattress because my mother didn't allow such things for us girls, and I just knew he would marry me, and we could live happily ever after. After all, that's what happened in all the teen magazines I read. It didn't quite work out that way. He said it probably wasn't his anyway because I had been with lots of other guys. Nothing could have been further from the truth. Suddenly, I saw this person for what he really was, and he no longer seemed to be so attractive or kind. In my young, naive mind, I grasped the realization that he had only been with me for one reason. It had been convenient for him that my mom's religion prohibited me from attending ball games at school, movies, or any other activities that normal kids got to enjoy. He could attend all these things with other girls without me ever seeing him since I couldn't go to any of them. I had few friends because of working in the fields, and the A&W drive-in job, so how could anyone in school even know about our cruising after work? It wasn't like I could call a girlfriend on the telephone and tell her all about it; hell, we didn't even have a phone. He had a perfectly good reason for only cruising with me and ultimately ending up in the back seat in the country. I was an isolated kid; he knew it and took full advantage of it.

Little did I know at the time that he would repeat this thirty-four years later and cost me the respect and love of my son as well as the loss of my two grandchildren for many years. My son's wife got on the Internet, located him, and planned for her and my son to go visit his brother, Jim, in Corcoran. My son told me later that when Jim opened the door, his wife had to take a step or two backwards because of his resemblance to my son. He looked so much like Danny's brother. Her words to my son were, "I know now what you will look like at fifty years old." The contact continued between my son, his wife, Danny, and his family. One night while standing out front of my son's house, I cautioned him to be careful of Danny; it was certainly his right to find him, meet him and even get to know him, but to be cautious. Without trying to make Danny look bad, I reminded him that he had ran out on me while I was pregnant with his child and then told terrible rumors about me around town. I had found out only too late that he was an evil, deceitful person who only looked after himself. As it turns out, Danny had two other children born to unwed mothers within a year after I gave birth to our son. I honestly believe my daughter-in-law always thought we were all right, knowing we loved her like a daughter, but after Danny's visit to Casa Grande, it all changed. She no longer wanted *my kind* around the children.

According to the good book, people will have to reap ten times what they have sown. Danny died of cancer in May 2000. God dealt with him harshly for the pain he had caused me by lying about being my son's father. Unfortunately, I still deal with the mess he created before his death. I spent months trying to figure out how he managed to have the DNA test, which he convinced my son to have done, show he wasn't my son's father. We all know DNA is conclusive and I simply couldn't figure it all out. Finally, I spoke with two different nurses, whom I've known for years, asking them how this was possible. I was told by more than one nurse, "Everything is for sale for the right price," even blood from a nurse's own arm and/or a swab from the mouth to replace that of the person giving a sample for DNA. What a sick society we live in. I've often wondered how a person could live with themselves after doing such a thing. Did it ever cross their minds the heartache and pain they may have caused someone by earning a few extra bucks switching their blood or swab for that of the donor being tested? Did they ever think about grandparents not being allowed to see their grandchildren again because they decided to assist in falsifying a DNA sample from the father...and for money of all things! God help them!

Going back to Corcoran at the ripe old age of 16, when my mom had found out I was pregnant she just cried, then said she had to tell my father. I had written a note to my friend, Sissy, in Casa Grande telling her I was pregnant, not knowing who else to turn to, left it on the fireplace for mother to mail and she opened it. R.C. hit the ceiling and called me all kinds of terrible names, while beating the crap out of me. RC said he always knew I was nothing but a whore and should never had allowed me to go to school or take the job at A&W. He called Danny at his house from a pay phone and told him he had to come out there right away. As he yelled at us both, he had a fireplace poker in his hand, and I wasn't sure just which one of us he was going to use it on, but Danny didn't stay around long enough to find out. He ran like the coward he was.

Two days later, my brother Joe showed up. He and R.C. discussed the back-alley abortion I was going to have up north in San Jose where Joe was evidentially scamming folks these days. R.C. wanted to know how long it would

take before I could get back to work in the fields after an
abortion. I told them both I wasn't having an abortion and
that I was going to continue to go to school, get my education, and raise my own child. It was the first time I had ever
actually stood up to R.C., and it was amazing I didn't have a
miscarriage after the beating I took from him for standing
my ground. Joe told me it wasn't an option, so I left in the
middle of the night and ran away. I called my mom at her
friend's house several days later and made her promise she
wouldn't let Joe and R.C. do this to my child. She promised
and told me Joe had already left. He probably had bigger
problems to attend or someone to scam somewhere else.

I continued to attend school but refused to work in the
fields. I helped mom can food and other household duties.
R.C. pretended I didn't exist. He went months without ever
looking or even talking to me. I considered it a blessing. My
grades improved because I had so much study time. Trust
me, in 1965 girls didn't go to school pregnant as they do
now, but I did. I was determined to get an education.

All the other students just stared at me, as I went from
class to class. It really didn't change my social life because I
never had one to start with. I was always just the poor, ugly
girl that lived outside of town. The school year ended in
May, and my son was born in July, so I was damn pregnant
by the end of the semester. Trust me ... it took true grit to
continue school with the public humiliation. However, I had
endured it my entire life due to the criminal activity of my
father and brothers, but this time, I had to take responsibility for my actions. I did it and was secretly proud of myself
for enduring it all and continuing my education.

I have never forgotten the humiliation and shame of attending school pregnant and made the decision in my own heart to help other girls when the time came. Up until just a few of years ago, I worked with young girls in high school who were unwed mothers. I would meet with them during lunch break when they came to the Baptist Church nearby to tend to the children. I would work with them and encourage them to stay in school, get that education, and not be dependent on anyone for anything except themselves and most importantly, be able to financially take care of their child. They, of course, knew nothing about my history, but I always marveled at how common it was for them to be in school pregnant and how times had changed. When it happened to me, I was the only girl in high school who was pregnant and stood out like a sore thumb, and the subject to cruel gossip and comments. When I started working with young, unwed mothers, I would go early to the Baptist Church to work with the girls, and leave after all of them had returned to school, as I never wanted any of them to see my car and never wore jewelry except for gold hoop earrings that could look like something bought in K-Mart. However, one day two of the girls were behind the church smoking and saw me get into my car. One walked up and said "You bitch, you act like you know what we're going through, and all the time you got this good life with an expensive car, etc." I asked them if they wanted to go for a late lunch, as it was apparent, they had no plans to return to school. I told them a condensed version of my life, being pregnant at such an early age, and how nobody went to school pregnant in those times. I explained to both that education was important to me and was how I ended up with the life I have and why I volunteer time to help and encourage others like themselves. I've stayed in touch with both girls over the years; they both graduated high school, and yes, I attended their graduations and they shared how much that had meant to them. One went onto college, and both are successful by today's standards, leaving me to believe I should have been more honest with all the girls I volunteered to help in that little Baptist Church, as perhaps it would have made a difference in their lives as well.

Although I was pregnant, mother and I could never have a conversation relating to childbirth because it just wasn't right for her to have this adult discussing with such a young girl who wasn't married. She was always uncomfortable discussing anything related to sex and after all, I was an unwed mother to be.

I suppose she thought if we didn't talk about it maybe it would go away. I never remember her acknowledging that I was pregnant. One of the do-gooders from the church wanted to give me a baby shower, but R.C. wouldn't hear of it. He told my mother that no daughter of his was going to get pregnant and give him another mouth to feed then get to have a baby shower and receive gifts. I thought it sounded like a damn good idea since I didn't have very much for this child who was due any day now.

The day my son was born, I sat on the edge of the bed combing my hair early in the morning, and I started getting what I thought was menstrual cramps. I had read all the books about childbirth, but I didn't understand everything I read and nobody to ask.

I remember they kept saying repeatedly in the books to go to the hospital when your pains are 8-10 minutes apart. Mine started at six then continued down to one minute apart. I went into the kitchen where mom was cooking and told her I thought something was wrong because the pains were going the wrong way. I thought they had to work their way up to 8-10 minutes apart, I didn't realize they went the other way. I knew absolutely nothing about childbirth.

When the realization hit mom that my pains were one minute apart it dawned on that her, she might be delivering this child. She immediately went to get R.C. Oh boy! This was just not what I wanted or needed at this time. The pains were frequent and hard, and I felt I could handle it all, if only I didn't have to deal with R.C. We drove to the hospital quickly, not because he cared whether I lived or died; he just didn't want a mess in his truck. At first, he told me I'd have to ride in the back of his truck, till mother reminded him I was pregnant, in labor and couldn't crawl up into the bed of the truck. By the time we reached the front desk, I was in hard labor. The admitting nurse took me to lie down on a bed right near her office and that's exactly where he was born. There wasn't time for all the prep stuff they did in those days when giving birth. I remember R.C. saying really loud that at least he wouldn't have to pay for anesthetic since the kid was born so fast. His only concern was for the hospital bill and another mouth to feed.

When the nurse came in the following morning to check everything, she informed me the stitches looked good. I went hysterical! What stitches? I assumed R.C. had convinced the doctor to sew me up so I could never get pregnant again. They had to give me a shot to calm me down. I heard later how it cost R.C. $7.50 for that damn shot. Later that day, they brought in this beautiful little boy. I was so scared, as I had never held a baby before. He appeared to smile at me to assure me we'd be fine. It was at this moment that I knew I had to leave R.C.'s house and start my life on my own. God, I was so young! How could I work, take care of this precious little baby, and go to school at the same time? I didn't know at that moment, but I knew I had to do this.

There were complications that hindered my plans to immediately go out into the big world and start my life. Apparently, the doctor had not removed all the after birth, and a serious infection started. I almost died. It was weeks before I could even function. By the time we were both ready for our six-week check-up, I could take him myself. While waiting in the lobby, I ran into Danny's sister-in-law who wanted to see my son. She asked me how I came up with a name, and I informed her my mother named him from the Bible. She whispered almost to herself, "He looks so much like Danny." I ignored this comment and proudly took my son into the doctor's office as my name was called.

After my son was born some of the do-gooders at the church brought small gifts so they could get into the door and view the unwed mother and child firsthand. And these people wonder why people don't flock their church doors. Amazing! Mother and I snuck around at secondhand stores and found some neat stuff. I had no idea how much a baby would use. Up until the time I became a young mother, I had never even held a baby before. But after his birth and I looked into his little face, I knew then that my life had to take a positive direction and that I would be the best mother I knew how to be.

Chapter 9
Leaving RC's House
after My Son's Birth

Amazing how much smarter we often seem to get with age. I've learned over the years, growing up with my family, to never, ever use the term "It can't get worse."

While looking for work, I met an exceptionally kind woman named Hester. Star is the meaning of the name Hester, and she was surely that to me. She owned a little restaurant situated outside Hanford, California. This little restaurant catered to mostly farmers in the area and appeared to be family-oriented, clean, and had sort of that homey atmosphere. I had stopped there to use their pay phone to call on another ad when I met her. She told me she was looking for a waitress and that I appeared to her to be friendly and smart. I never had anyone tell me before I was "smart looking," so I immediately took to her.

When Hester hired me, I explained somewhat my situation but altered the truth just a bit by telling her my husband was in the service and was stationed overseas and that I had a small child. It didn't seem like such a bad lie, and in 1965 you simply didn't advertise that you were an out-of-wedlock mother. I also had purchased a small, cheap wedding band that confirmed my lie and served another purpose as well ...it kept the wolves away since they thought I was married. I eventually told her the truth, although I think she had figured it all out when the "overseas letters" didn't come from my invented husband.

She never told a soul, but occasionally there were some who came from Corcoran that knew. They would always whisper and look at me, but since life was so good, or at least to me it was because I didn't have to tolerate R.C., I had a job, a home, and my precious little boy. I simply couldn't resist being almost arrogant to them at times.

She lived in a house right out back and was willing to have me and my young son stay with her in her spare bedroom. Things were totally looking up. I couldn't wait to get that old Ford headed for Corcoran, get my few belongings, including my son, and move in and start working. I was concerned about school since now I would be working full-time but decided I could take some correspondence courses and work on them at night while my son played or slept. Having a social life wasn't something I wanted or even considered. I thought I had men all figured out; between my brothers, R.C. and Danny, I had decided they only wanted one thing, and it wasn't going to happen to me again. I felt so focused and excited. It was my time to grow up and move on. After all, I never had much of a childhood anyway.

I was sixteen, a mother, and proud of the fact I had landed not only a job but a nice place for my son and I to live. What happened to me next wasn't part of the plan.

It was as though R.C. already knew. How could he possibly know? Nobody knew except for me and Hester. When I drove up to the house, his truck was parked right in front; he was waiting for me. "Where in the hell have you been, out getting yourself pregnant again? You can get the hell out of my house right now, but this kid is staying here with your mother and I."

No...no...no was all I could think. When I told him I had a job and a place to live, he informed me he didn't care if I lived in the street, but I wasn't taking the kid anywhere. I pleaded to my mother, unfortunately; she could never stand up to R.C. She backed him up 100 percent because they had become attached to this little guy and didn't want to give him up. Too bad! He was mine, and I was determined to raise him with better morals than R.C. could instill in him.

After a terrible argument, I finally agreed to let him stay with them, or at least make them think I had agreed and started gathering my things. Mother was trying to be kind by giving me some old towels and a pillow. All I could think of was "You're giving me this shit, yet you're keeping my son." I don't ever remember being so disappointed in my mother. My mind just kept going back to all those trips to visit this asshole in prison, and now she was backing him up on this.

I put all my things in my old Ford and quietly gathered my son's things and thought I could make it out the door with both. R.C. was waiting by the front door and knocked me completely back into the living room. mother ran and picked up my son and asked him not to hit me like that. He told me if I ever came around again, he would kill me and bury me right out there, pointing to the fields, and that nobody would ever know. Unfortunately for me, the more he talked, the madder he got, and when mother left the room with my son and went into the kitchen, he physically kicked me out the front door and continued beating me until I thought he would have a heart attack. At least I kept hoping he would drop dead because I simply didn't know how much more of this I could take. He knew mother would call him off he if did this inside which is why he waited until kicking me out the front door. I kept thinking if I screamed loud enough, she would hear me, I knew she did ... yet she never came back out to help me.

When I got back to Hanford, I looked like I had been in a car wreck, which is the story Hester and I decided to stay with for customers in the restaurant. She even laughed and said, "The old farm boys who come in here will feel sorry for you and tip better". She was rather resourceful. Two weeks went by, I worked long hours at the restaurant, ordered my correspondence courses and cried myself to sleep at night because I missed my son so much. Sometimes at night after we cleaned the restaurant, I would get creative and start cooking some old country dishes in the kitchen like stew, cornbread, and such. It was something to do, and the "Daily Specials" were ready for the next day.

I knew mother went to church every Sunday night, and I decided to catch her in the parking lot before she went in. The restaurant was always closed on Sundays, so I went early to make sure I didn't miss her. I convinced her I could and would take care of my own son and what R.C. did wasn't right. She agreed but said she didn't know what else to do. I told her about the beating in the front yard and still had some bruising on my back, arms, and legs but I could tell she didn't want to believe this.

She informed me R.C. was going to Tulare the next day and would be gone almost all day. Probably had a girlfriend over there, but mother insisted it was business. She agreed to let me have my son but said she would have to tell R.C.

that I stole him away while she was hanging laundry on the clothesline or something else while she was outside. I agreed. I would have agreed to almost anything to get my son back. The plan worked, and I went and got him the following day. He had the biggest smile, and I could tell he was happy to see his Mama, even at such an early age.

Only taking about a week for RC to find where I worked and lived after taking my son. He used to go into town in the mornings at the coffee shop and after asking around found someone that told him where I worked and that he thought I lived with Hester behind the restaurant. When he walked through that door, I thought I would die. Lunchtime was always busier than hell, but I knew I had to run to the house and get my son from the babysitter. I grabbed him, his playpen, and put him into the kitchen, then went back out front and waited on my customers. Hester knew what was going on and immediately went over and told him she knew the damn Tisons and wasn't going to put up with any of his shit and that if he created a problem, she would have him arrested. I wasn't even aware that she knew anything about my family; apparently, she did but was kind enough not to ever bring it up. About that time, two officers came in for lunch, and he slithered out like the snake that he was. I knew him well enough to know he'd be back and probably bringing Joe with him, so I just took a lot of precautions. From that day, my son was rarely out of my sight.

Hester was in her forties, long hair pulled back and tied with a ribbon. She had an easy smile and a laid-back personality, and I knew we would be friends for a long time to come, which we were. She sort of looked like an old folk singer. Of course, at sixteen, anyone over the age of twenty-five looked old to me. As it turned out, she did play the guitar, and we spent countless evenings sitting under a tree out back singing old gospel tunes and watching my son play in a playpen that I had picked up at a used furniture store.

She had graduated high school and taken some college courses, so of course I thought she was smart. When I'd get stuck on something with my correspondence classes, she would always help me out. What a great, long-time friend she turned out to be. I've always believed that God has put me right where I needed to be and Guardian Angels around me. Was surely no accident that I stopped at her restaurant that day to use to pay phone .. another Guardian Angel the Good Lord sent me.

Several months later, she asked if I'd like to go to a concert because her cousin, Roger Miller, had sent her some tickets. I thought she was joking about Roger Miller being her cousin, but I went anyway. After the show, we went backstage and met him, and he took us to dinner. I just kept thinking life couldn't get any better than this...I had taken my son to a babysitter in Hanford who had come highly recommended by one of my customers, so if RC came by the house, nobody would be there. I learned to take a lot of precautions, as I knew he was always going to harass me.

Chapter 10
Marrying and Living with Abuse Again

I met and married a guy who I thought was the man of my dreams. Surely didn't take all that long to realize I had married an abuser and womanizer, much like my father. However, in my young mind I was sure if I were a good enough wife, cooked, and catered to him, he would change. I was wrong but stayed for many years tolerating the physical and emotional abuse. He was in the Army, and we were able to travel and live-in places I had only heard about while growing up in Casa Grande. Nothing was ever good enough for him. He wouldn't allow me to use a broom and mop, so he had a bucket and rags and woke me up an hour earlier than he and the kids, so I could scrub the floors on my hands and knees. He insisted they were cleaner this way for the children to play on.

After being stationed for several years in Europe, we came back to the United States and were stationed in Mc-Kees Rocks, Penn. We lived in a government-leased house in a development outside Pittsburg for almost a year then the military relocated us to Key West, Florida, where he also lived in a leased house off base. I never had a choice in where we lived and would have preferred living on base, where I could perhaps have friends and the kids be able to play with other children. I finally realized by living off base, which he always arranged, he wasn't worried about being caught for being abusive and beating me. Even then, physical abuse by a spouse was against U.S. Army standards and was not tolerated. Unfortunately for me, I was far too scared to ever report him for the abuse and beatings, as I knew it would only be worse for me, much like growing up with RC and brothers.

Raymond liked fast cars and liked working on them, so he entered our GTO (his car) into drag races being held at Pittsburgh International Raceway. I once asked if I could drive in the Powder Puff races and after begging, he finally agreed for a one-time race. I did good and won $250 which was a fortune for us at the time. He used the money to work on the GTO and I kept racing since my times were so much better than his, of course we never said this out loud. After months of racing and winning money, the Pittsburgh Press decided to do an article on me reading "Life's a Big Drag .. But She's Got Drive" showing a picture of my three kids sitting in the stands watching Mama race. I was so thrilled that I tore the entire front page off and put it on the wall in our kitchen. After the kids went to bed that night, I took one hell of a beating for being so boastful about the article as he said he only let me drive because he felt sorry for me, not that I was really any good at it. We both knew that wasn't true as I could double clutch, shift gears and ran much better than himself, but I agreed with him as always. He tore the article up, but I obtained another copy and after all these years, my daughter still has it in a frame.

The few friends I had which were also military dependents, thought we were so lucky to have such a nice house off base. Little did they know why we lived such an isolated life off base; they had no idea the abuse I was tolerating, and he always beat me where it wouldn't show when dressed. Other wives used to get together and go on tours and such, but this was out of the question for me, as Raymond didn't approve and didn't think I needed friends since I had he and the kids to care for. I started taking college classes when living outside Pittsburg and continued in Key West. It took a lot of effort, but I convinced Raymond that when he left the military, if I had a college degree, even though it was going to take a while to get, that I could help him support our family. Since it benefited him, he finally agreed. One of the first classes I took along with others was psychology. I loved it and was beginning to understand in my own young mind that I had married the likes of my father and brothers – he was abusive, controlling, and had a sexual appetite that couldn't be filled. Of course, I never told Raymond that I was taking psychology classes and hid my homework and assignments on these classes from him. I also managed to erase them off my entrance paperwork, so he never knew that was the beginning of my future without him.

Shortly after we were relocated to Key West, my father passed away while living in Tulsa, Oklahoma, with my mother. My brother Joe had called me to tell me and that I needed to come for the funeral. I reminded him that RC and I had fought our entire lives and why would I leave a one-year-old baby and two small children to travel for his funeral. I also reminded him we had no money for a plane ticket. He said he had already spoken with the Red Cross, and they would buy me a ticket there, and he would pay for the returning ticket. His offering to pay for a return ticket didn't set well in my heart, while setting off *red flags* in my head, as Joe never did anything that didn't benefit himself or come with strings attached. He assured me my mother needed me to be there with her and that if I loved her, I'd "get my ass on a plane." He said that all I had to do was contact the local Red Cross to finalize, as he had already made the initial contact for me. My love for my mother was strong, and I did want to be there for her.

I arranged for someone to care for my kids while Raymond was on duty and hitched a ride on a military bus to the airport in Miami. Key West was the last island southeast of Miami, a hundred plus miles away.

Once arriving in Tulsa, looking at my mother's broken spirit and heart, I was glad I had come. Though I never understood it, she loved RC with all her heart and soul and was going to be lost without him. It was awkward for me though during the visitation and service as I had nothing to say – good, bad, or indifferent – about my father. He was a mean, cruel person who chased women and the almighty buck and was never successful at the latter. I just sort of faded into the surroundings except for sitting with my mother outside quietly for what seemed like hours. She told me numerous times about how happy she was that I had come to be with her and was so happy Joe was paying for my plane ticket home; she even managed to tell me a couple times what a good boy he was, I let it go as I had so many times before. I still had serious reservations about his offer to do this and wondered what the price I would have to pay for it, as I knew with Joe there was always a catch. I just didn't know what it was until we left to the airport.

We made small talk in his El Camino on the ride to the airport, but he said he needed to make a stop, wouldn't take long but he would need my help .... OK here it comes ... the catch. I reminded him I had three small children at home in Key West and needed to get on a plane as quickly as possible.

We stopped in front of a small neighborhood-type cocktail and billiards lounge. He explained what was going to happen when we went in and said bluntly that if I didn't help him, I would be hitchhiking back to Key West. My heart kept skipping beats, as I thought he was going to rob the place ... although I think that would have been easier than what happened. First, he reminded me that "Betsy," his sawn-off shot gun, was under his seat, but we probably wouldn't need it; he just wanted to make sure I knew it was there in case we did. Oh shit, I was more terrified by the moment as he kept talking. He explained that he was an exceptional pool player and that I was going to go in first and sit at the bar and have a drink. He gave me a couple of hundred-dollar bills to wager. I seriously thought of taking that two hundred and running like hell but didn't think it was enough for a plane ticket. He probably knew that, too, which is why he didn't give me more. He would come in within a few minutes, but I was to act as though I didn't know him. He planned to hustle those playing and after a couple of games of losing, he wanted me to wager a rather large amount on him, as if I was drunk and didn't know any better. He reminded me again that the winnings were my plane ticket home, and it was this or hitchhiking.

I was terrified but did what he said, all the time praying for God to protect me and get me out of there safely and back to my children. I did exactly as he had asked and thought I'd done good until he won over a thousand dollars, and I jumped up and said, "Good job Joe." At this point, the other players realized they had been hustled and decided they were going to take care of us. Joe explained, almost begging, explained that I was his younger sister, was a military dependent who had come for our father's funeral, and he had forced me to do this. He begged them to let me go which fortunately, they did. However, as I started to walk out the front door Joe yelled, "Please tell Betsy I love her." Holy shit! I knew he meant the sawn-off shot gun and wasn't sure exactly what he wanted me to do with it, but I knew he wanted that gun.

As I ran outside the lounge, I stood there taking deep breaths, then started throwing up, which I had done so many times before being in situations with them, and the thought of hitchhiking from Tulsa back to Key West was sounding better by the moment in my head. I finally walked to his truck, took the gun out from under the seat, and stood there for a while trying to remember where they were all standing when I had run out the door. Finally, with all the courage I could muster, I flung open the door and with hands on both ends of the shotgun, flung it through the air at Joe. He immediately cocked it, facing the others, and picked up all the money laying on the bar and instructed me to go start the truck. I couldn't get out of there quick enough, as I was sure we were all going to die as this son of a bitch was crazier than I'd ever realized. He immediately came running out a few seconds behind me and said, "Drive as fast as you can." He surely didn't have to tell me twice, as I was terrified and just felt lucky to be alive at this point. After a few blocks, he told me to pull over, got in the driver's seat, and drove to the airport. He asked me which airline I had booked a flight on, and I looked at him like he was nuts. "Seriously!" I almost screamed. "I hadn't booked anything because you told me you'd get me home." He stopped in front of one of the airlines, gave me $300 and told me to get the fuck out of the truck. As I learned early in life not to ever say "It can't get worse" because in my family, it always did, and this was surely one of those times.

I grabbed my small bag from the backseat and jumped out before Joe could change his mind and come up with some other crazy idea to make more money by using me. My entire body was shaking all over, as I walked inside the airport and walked up and asked an agent at the ticket counter if I could buy a flight to Miami with $300. Luckily, I could, and they had a flight leaving within an hour. I've never been happier to leave anywhere in my life than I was Tulsa at the time. I called Raymond collect before boarding the plane and told him what time I would arrive in Miami. He said if he couldn't make it, just take the military bus. I kept thinking, if only he knew what I'd just lived through, he would be waiting for me with open arms to comfort me and want to keep me safe. However, in my heart, I knew he was so much like my father and brothers, he wouldn't do anything that didn't benefit himself.

I sat next to some older man on the flight, and he wanted to chat. I just wanted to quietly pray and thank God I was away from Joe, those bad guys at that lounge and on the way home to my babies. The gentleman next to me had ordered a dinner, and it smelled so good, I was almost nauseated; I hadn't paid for one when purchasing the ticket as it was another $12, which I didn't have. I couldn't remember when I'd last eaten and was starving. As he was unwrapping his plasticware, he apparently somehow realized I hadn't or couldn't pay for the meal, he placed his dinner onto my pull-down tray and said he wasn't hungry and asked if I wanted it. I remember thinking, "God continually puts angels in my life to protect and keep me." I ate every bite, maybe even licking the plasticware. I drifted off to sleep while in silent prayer, knowing I would be with my babies soon.

Of course, Raymond wasn't at the airport. I waited hours for a military bus heading to Key West and then walked from the base to our house, as Raymond said he didn't hear the phone ring. Right! All I could think of was that I was so happy that gentleman next to me gave me his dinner so at least I wasn't hungry.

As I look back over my life, I realize that God has always taken care of me and for that, I'm grateful daily and still thankful to my mother for instilling such faith in God in me.

I had lived with verbal, physical, and psychological abuse far too long with Raymond. We, as a society, and those who work in the mental health field, now understand the cycle of abuse, but I surely didn't know anything about it then. I had married a man who was like my father and brothers – physically and verbally abusive, the same type people I thought I was escaping. Had I known then what I now know, I would have walked away, no, I would have run away from this abuser. But little did I know at the time and with small children to raise, I felt trapped and afraid to do anything except stay and take it.

It started when he was stationed at Ft. MacArthur Military Base in San Pedro, Calif., and got progressively worse in El Paso, Texas, and increasingly worse while we were stationed in Germany. He was assigned to a Vulcan Chap-arral unit while in Texas. These weapons would shoot 6,000 rounds per minute and, at least in my opinion, looked like the old cannons used in the Civil War. I would drive my two sons out to White Sands, New Mexico, to watch them practice while we were stationed in El Paso, Texas. The military was preparing to take the entire unit along with guns to Germany. They had been used during the Vietnam War, however, due to the humidity, they rusted and didn't fire accurately. The U.S. Army decided to experiment with them in Germany. Although the winters were cold and wet from snow, the humidity was low. Since this was an experi-mental program, the soldiers spent a great deal of time in the field, rarely being home with their families. In my case, considering how physically abusive Raymond had become, this was a blessing.

The pressure on this unit was great, as all the wives learned. When we finally arrive in Europe, little did we know about PTSD then, only that this type of duty was taking its toll on our husbands, even though it wasn't com-bat. Arriving at the Frankfurt Airport, Raymond decided to travel with the troops rather than fly with me or take me and the boys to the place off base that had been rented for us. My God, I was in a foreign country, I didn't speak the language, and my youngest son was sick with pneumonia. A priest had helped me with him on the long flight over and allowed me to periodically rest, however he left immediate-ly after arriving at the airport. I had an oxygen bag hanging on one shoulder, a sick child in the other, and was dragging the older one behind.

We spent hours going through customs. The building

had no air conditioner, and it was hot, and my boys kept taking their clothes off despite my continuously putting them back on. We finally made it through customs and went outside to find a military deuce and half trucks were our transportation. We were assisted by military personnel putting ourselves and bags into the back, and I kept telling the boys how fun this experience was going to be while being terrified in my heart.

We arrived in the village of Bad Kreuznach, hours from Frankfurt where we had landed, and where an upstairs apartment waited for us. It was the upstairs of a German family's homes that had been converted into an apartment. In Germany, at this time, they close the shutters on the windows at night, and this village had no streetlights. When the soldier started unloading my bags and helped the boys and I down, my heart sunk, as I was terrified. I rang the bell, and a woman who I often referred to as a white-looking Aunt Jemima came to the door. I immediately said what I had been practicing in Deutsche, "Hello and it's nice to meet you." She continued to speak, and I started crying and said, "That's all the Deutsche I know."

She laughed and said, "Good thing I speak perfectly good English then." You can't possibly imagine what a relief that was to me .... yet another Angel in my life. She insisted on taking the kinders (children) upstairs and helped me put them to bed, asking them if they were hungry, which they were. She fed us all, and we slept like babies. I felt safe with Frau Myer. We became great friends, even after I returned to the United States, communicating through letters until her death. She took an immediate dislike to Raymond once she heard him knocking me around, once telling me I should hit him over the head with a pan. I was never brave enough to do that, but sure did think about it a lot.

Often when he was home, he drank excessively, and one night he slapped me so hard I fell against a wall. All I could think of was "What in the hell am I going to do, I'm a million miles from home, don't speak the language, and living in the upstairs apartment of a German family." I did feel a certain amount of safety there with Frau Meyer right downstairs; I felt if it got too bad, I could run down to her. There wasn't even a telephone, to make calls; we had to go to the military base and by road it was twelve miles away, however by country roads it was only a couple of miles straight up the mountain. Neither was a choice for me that night as I knew he would never let me leave. It escalated over the years even though when he sobered up, he would cry and promise never to do it again. He once told me he would cut his hands off before ever physically hurting me again, although that only lasted until he got drunk again. We, as a society, didn't understand at that point about the cycle of abuse, or PTSD, only that we, as abused women normally were attracted to what we thought we never wanted to be a part of. Considering the abuse of my childhood from my father and brothers, I felt as though I wanted to run as far away from this lifestyle as possible. However, I followed the pattern of "they cycle of abuse" and married the likes of my father.

When I became pregnant with DeAnna, he didn't hit me for fear of hurting the baby. It was wonderful for a while, but in the back of my mind I knew I shouldn't push him at all when he was drinking. It didn't take long after her birth for him to resume his physical abuse. He would often tell me how fat and ugly I was, which is why he turned to other women. Unlike being the ugly duckling, I was while growing up, I had developed into an attractive woman, weighing about 105 lbs., anything but fat. I walked for exercise long before we knew it was healthy to do so and used music to exercise in the house when nobody was around. I absolutely loved this man and wanted to be the best possible, attractive wife I could be. I wanted to be someone he could be proud of and to not want other women. I was a good mother, an excellent housekeeper as it was required since I didn't work while stationed in El Paso and Germany. He didn't even allow me to use a broom; I had to do the floors daily on my hands and knees, as he felt like the broom and mop didn't get it clean enough for the kids to play on. When home, he would set his alarm an hour early so he could wake me up to do the floors before he and the kids got up. I always cooked his favorite meals and had turned into quite a good cook with practice. Little did I know at the time, it didn't matter what I looked like or did, he was a womanizer, just like my father, he chased women our entire married life. One of the first things I did when I left him was buy a broom and a mop. Somehow it was like saying "Look at me asshole, I can do whatever now."

After returning to the United States one night, I got a babysitter and went onto the military base when we were stationed in Key West on my little Yamaha 175, which was the only vehicle I could afford gas for, and found him sitting with two beautiful women at the club, drinking cocktails, laughing, and having a good time. I walked up to the table and said, "I don't care what you do, who you party with, or even who you sleep with, but I need milk money for the kids." Ouch, it didn't take long for those two women to walk away, realizing what a loser he was for his kids not having milk money. He had probably told them he was divorced or never married or whatever his story was. I got onto my bike and went home. In my heart, I knew I had gone too far with him and knew I was going to pay for it, but at the same time, I was laughing inside thinking he would be the subject of many jokes in that club in the future and would have to find another place to drink and pick up women.

He came home shortly after that, and I knew he was mad. The kids were in bed asleep, and he put the two dogs he had trained to protect us into a bedroom and closed the door. He turned on the TV, which he often did, as the kids had learned to sleep through the noise. He found me in the kitchen and proceeded to punch me in the face, the stomach, and everywhere else it seemed. There were so many punches, I lost count ... not that I was counting. He was no longer hitting me where it wouldn't show when dressed; he was completely out of control and hitting me all over. At some point I heard my jaw crack, knowing full well he had broken it. I could hear the dogs barking and scratching at the door, and I kept calling their names as I had nobody else to call. They eventually chewed through the hollow core door and came after him. Unfortunately, he had done a tremendous amount of damage before they got to me. I seriously gave thought to letting them chew him up until I came to my senses and got them by the collars and pulled them off him. They had chewed him up good for hurting me but nothing a Band-Aid wouldn't fix, or so I thought.

I had to call an ambulance because I was in real bad shape and felt certain that my jaw was broken since I could

hardly speak, and it hurt more than childbirth. I also realized I was bleeding quite a bit, but there were so many injuries that I wasn't quite sure where the blood was coming
from. Speaking was difficult, but I was able to give them my
address and ask them to rush. I also asked them to send the
Military Police as we were a military family. When they
arrived with red lights and sirens, the neighbors of course,
all came out to see what was going on. Raymond immediately met them at the door and told them his beautiful wife
had been attacked by someone who broke into our home
while he was on duty and that he had walked in on it and
that his injuries were a result of him fighting off the
attacker. I could tell from the look on one of the EMTs that
he wasn't buying this and requested Military Police be
rushed to the scene, possibly as he thought he may also be
in danger. As he started to administer treatment to me, he
asked "Who did this to you?" Without hesitation, I said "my
husband" pointing toward Raymond. There was no way I
was going to allow him to get away with this, not this time,
not as bad as it was, and my injuries were far worse than I
even knew at the time. The military officer asked about the
children and if I had anyone, I could contact to stay with
them, as they were going to take Raymond into custody. I
told them that I did not, Raymond had kept me isolated
from others, so I had no friends, so they contacted the
Provost Marshalls office and had a nurse come. I refused to
go into the ambulance until I knew my children were going
to be cared for. The beautiful nurse held my hand and
assured me she would take good care of my children for me.
Except for going to school and working at a Latin officer's
Club on Friday and Saturday nights as a Bartender, I was

always with them and felt they would be confused when waking up and finding I was gone. I kept begging the nurse to hug them and assure them everything was going to be fine and to please not tell them what had happened. I would find a way to explain to them later.

A military caseworker was assigned to me while I was still in the emergency room, and she asked about family she could contact to come and stay with my children long term as I was in bad shape and probably be there for quite a while. I gave her my mother's phone number. R.C. had died, so he wouldn't prevent her from coming to be with me and my children. The Red Cross bought her a ticket, and she was there the following day; a Military Officer picked her up at Miami Airport and brought to Key West. She walked right past my room several times, looking in but not recognizing me, as I was so savagely beaten. Finally, when the nurse directed her into the room, she broke down into tears. No one would give me a mirror, so I had no idea of just how bad I looked. My face was swollen to almost twice its size, my jaw was wired together on the inside, so that explained why I had so much trouble talking, I had numerous broken ribs, cuts and bruises, and stitches everywhere it seemed. I didn't even recognize myself when I finally did look in a mirror. My hip was also dislocated so I walked with a cane for a couple years. I was in intensive care unit at the Key West Military Hospital for several weeks and then a regular hospital room for another few weeks. Mother and I had decided to tell the kids that I had been in a car accident rather than tell them the truth. Little did I know that my boys knew all the time but let me have my peace of thinking they hadn't been subject to something so violent.

Out of nowhere, Joe showed up at the hospital after a couple of weeks. I'm sure mother had called him to tell him what had happened. I couldn't believe this and couldn't help but wonder why he was there or if he even cared because he surely never did before. I'll never forget how happy mother was when he walked into the room, saying "Oh look Lynda, your brother Joe is here to see you." I suppose I was supposed to be thrilled; however, my mind immediately went to "What the hell does he want and how can he benefit from this?" All I could think of was what he had put me through in Tulsa just to get home. I wasn't being negative; this is what and who he was, and I knew it. I often wondered if mother ever actually knew what/who they were or is love for your children truly so blind? I never told her about the incident in Tulsa because I wasn't sure she would believe me, and it served no purpose at this point. She reminded me that he had flown all the way from Phoenix to Miami and rented a car and drove through the Keys all the way to Key West just to see his sister. Right!? I wasn't buying any of this, but I was so beaten up and weak I knew I had to concentrate on getting well enough to care for my children again.

Right after mother left with the kids to take them home after our daily visit, Joe wasted no time getting right to the point of his visit. He explained in detail that he had done some research and learned that a soldier with Raymond's rank and three children, had an insurance policy on him by the military for $25,000 and $50,000 for accidental death. The light bulb went off in my head, and I immediately knew why he was there. This was the brother I knew, not one who came to visit me because I had almost been beaten to death but because he saw dollar signs. I'm sure he had already figured out how to get this money from me once the military insurance paid out after he killed or had Raymond killed.

I was almost hysterical trying to explain to him through my mouth that was wired together that he couldn't do this, it wasn't right and that even though Raymond had made a terrible mistake when drunk and almost killed me, he couldn't kill him or have him killed, he just couldn't. He kept trying to explain how it would appear to be an accident, as it had to be for the military to pay the full double indemnity of $50,000, otherwise it would only be $25,000. I hit the button and called for the nurse and asked her through hysterical tears to please call my mother and have her come back to the hospital, which she did. I told her what Joe was planning to do, and she also told him he couldn't do this. She told him the military would take care of me and the kids and that he should leave. I couldn't believe my mother had stood up to Joe for me. I kept thinking how happy I was that Raymond had been restricted to base, at least he was safe from Joe. Even though mother and I both told him he could not possibly do this; I wasn't sure he would listen. Raymond wasn't in custody anymore but was restricted to the base. I knew Joe would never go onto a military base for any reason, so I assumed a certain amount of safety for Raymond; I'm not sure he deserved it, but he didn't deserve to die. After all, I had lived and even though it was going to take a long time, I would heal.

When I was finally released from the hospital, I had asked my mother to contact the base and have someone stay with the kids so she could come along. When we got into my little red Volkswagen that I had brought from Germany, I told her to take me to the Provost Marshall's Office on base. There was an officer at the door who helped me into a chair, as they knew I was coming in and the military lawyer quickly came out to take me into his office, offering his sincere apologies for what had happened to me, like it was his fault. He had the entire file as well as photos that were taken by the emergency room personnel and charges were pending against Raymond, so of course, he knew all the details of what happened that awful night. He questioned me about how long this abuse had been going on and I told him for years but was afraid to ever report him. He asked me what I needed from him, and I didn't hesitate to tell him … "I wanted to go home", through my wired together jaw. For all practical purposes, Casa Grande was the only home I'd known, and my mother was there. I reminded him that, the military brought me and my kids here and they needed to send me home. He quickly agreed and asked when I wanted to go assuring me Raymond would remain on restriction to base so I wasn't in any danger. I didn't hesitate to tell him, "I want to go yesterday." He chuckled a bit and then he got on the phone and arranged for a Bekins moving truck to be at my house the following morning to pack up everything and move me to Casa Grande. I explained to him I would have to find a job and a place to live once arriving home and my things would all need to remain in storage. He assured me the military would take care of all cost, and once I was settled to call Bekins and they would deliver everything at no charge to me.

Mother flew back to Phoenix the following day; the Provost Marshall's Office had arranged for a military officer to drive her from Key West to the mainland and catch a flight in Miami. The Red Cross flew my mother back to Phoenix and even though this was almost fifty years ago, I still contribute heavily to the Red Cross because of what they did for me in such a time of need. Someone from the church picked mother up at the airport in Phoenix. For the first time in years, I was happy to have all those Pentecostal's praying for me after walking out of the church at age 15. I needed all the help I could get from prayers. The church lady who picked mother up had a reputation of being a gossip, so I'm sure she was more than happy to have all the gossip about what happened firsthand and could share it with anyone who was listening. What had happened was surely bad enough, nobody needed to embellish, however by the time some of the stories got back to my mother they had grown a bit, she set them straight and moved on. Mother wasn't much for gossip and surely didn't like it when it was about her kids, even her boys. God knows there wasn't a lot left to image about my father and brothers as most of it was on the front page of newspapers or evening news.

I was shocked that the six men from Bekins Moving Company could pack an entire house up in one day, label everything so well, and get it on a truck to move me. I had mother help me pack bags for us to take with us before she left, and they were in the little red Volkswagen I had named "Charlie" for some unknown reason when I purchased her from a Canadian PX in Belgium. I planned to drive home with myself, three kids and two dogs. I rarely saw a Bekins truck for many years after that when I didn't think of how kind those six men were that packed my home up. They saw how bad of shape I was in, and one even asked me what happened. When I knew the kids were out of earshot, I told him my husband had gotten drunk and done this to me. He said, "Well that SOB, but please know we are going to take good care of you and get all your stuff safely to Arizona." I'm sure he shared this with the other movers, and they were exceptionally nice to me, seeming to take extra pains with all my belongings. One even went and brought back lunch and sodas and snacks for the kids. I was overwhelmed with their kindness and hugged and cried with each one of them, as they left with everything I owned on their truck.

The military lawyer had cut me a check for Raymond's pay for two months, and with a whopping few hundred dollars I was off the start my new life with my kids. I couldn't hardly wait to start putting miles between me and this abuser I had called "husband" for so long. After the movers left, we stayed in a motel the first night in Key West. We swam in the pool and had hamburgers and sodas and I talked to them about Casa Grande and what a wonderful place it was. Of course, the younger ones wanted to know if daddy was going to live there with us, somehow. I would answer them with a quick "I'm not sure yet."

Only taking one day of driving for me to realize it was far too hot to travel during the day even with the widows down, and Charlie didn't have A/C. We got all the way to a town outside New Orleans, and I got a motel and I decided I would sleep outside with the kids playing in the pool and drive at night when it was cooler. My boys were both excellent swimmers, and I explained to them that I was going to drive at night but needed to sleep a little during the day. They became my rock and assured me they would watch

DeAnna while I slept in a lawn chair by the pool and kept her safe. We took the dogs for a long run before starting out about dusk. By being in the pool most of the day, running with the dogs and dinner, they were tired enough to sleep, probably through the night. My Volkswagen didn't have a radio, so I sang. The kids thought I was good, but of course they were kids and loved their mom. About 2 a.m., I was getting so sleepy but knew I had to put miles behind me. I started singing praises, scriptures from the Bible I was taught as a child, and prayed for God to give me a peace, energy, and rest of my body. I still was in bad physical shape from the beating, but I felt I could do this. Strange how a mother's love can accomplish things we probably couldn't do alone.

The night seemed so black, perhaps not, perhaps it was in my mind, as I was feeling so alone and scared. I was feeling like I was out there in this old world all alone in the desert of Texas with three kids who trusted me to care for them, not to mention the two Boxer dogs, and I was alone. A car got behind me and started flashing their lights, and it frightened me as I was in such an isolated area of the Texas desert. I had noticed they had been following me for a while but assumed since we were all going the same direction, I didn't think it was too unusual until they started flashing their lights for me to pull over. I sped up and prayed they would go away. I saw a sign that read "Truck Stop" a few miles down the road and was so relieved and felt if I could get there with all the lights and such, I would be safe.

When I finally got to this truck stop, I pulled right up to the front door and felt we were safe. I grabbed my cane and got out of the car; I was pissed at these horrible people who had done this to me. They had pulled up right behind me, and I yelled at them as I walked up to their car and asked them what they wanted. It turned out it was an older couple, and the woman was almost in tears. They both got out of their car and told me they had seen me, the kids, and the dogs at our last stop. It was a coincidence that we were going the same way, however when I started weaving, was the reason they started flashing their lights. They had assumed I was tired and falling asleep at the wheel, which I was until they flashed their lights and scared the hell out of me. She said we noticed your military sticker on the car, which was why we were following me. They explained their son and only child had been killed fighting in the Vietnam War and that they wanted to help me. They asked if they could buy the kids and me breakfast. The old man helped me get the dogs out, put leashes on them and took them for a long run for me. I was so tired and worn out, I was grateful for his help with the dogs. I took the kids into the bathroom and washed their faces and changed their shirts and shorts and we met this older couple inside the restaurant. He had tied the dogs up outside where the kids and I could see them and had given them water and had even bought some extra dog food and a new pan and allowed them to eat as well. You would have had to live through a situation like this to appreciate how grateful I was for their help. I was extremely tired, recovering from injuries and alone with three kids in the middle of what seemed like nowhere. As I sat in the truck stop eating breakfast with these two people, I absolutely knew they were angels sent by God.

These angels of mercy told the kids they could have anything on the menu they wanted, and of course, they all wanted pancakes. I insisted they eat bacon as well so it would stick to their ribs, as mother used to say, and not be so hungry so quickly again. They thought this was cool to be eating breakfast at 3 a.m. in a truck stop. I never, ever would feed them sandwiches on the side of the road because I had such bad memories from having to do this with my mother on those horrible trips to see R.C. while he was in prison. My kids and I would usually eat in cheap mom and pop type restaurants and a couple times at Holiday Inns as they advertised "Kids Eat Free." Yippee, that was surely a plus. Never, though, would I feed my kids sandwiches on the side of the road. I had only a few hundred dollars and knew I had to rent a place to live once we arrived in Casa Grande, so I used each dollar wisely.

As we finished eating and walked outside to where the dogs were, and they wanted to talk to me while the kids were busy playing with the dogs. They apologized again for scaring me earlier, told me once again, the reason they had flashed their lights at me was because I was apparently going to sleep at the wheel and was weaving all over the road. It surely worked because I was so scared, I was then wide awake from fear. The lady handed me an envelope with cash in it and explained that their son had died while serving in the military, they had received compensation for his death, never using it, and they wanted to help me and to please take the envelope. She insisted it wasn't much but knew I had two days of traveling left to get to Casa Grande and that this would take care of hotels and food until we reached home. I was overwhelmed with their generosity but didn't want to take the envelope. The lady once again got tears in her eyes and said, "Please take this, as we really want to help you and you children; it would make us feel really good in our hearts, and we won't worry about you so much. We would follow you all the way home, but we live only twenty miles from here and our journey will be over." I took the envelope, hugged them both and assured them they were angels sent from heaven. When I opened the envelope, it had $500 in it and a check for another $500. I felt I had won the lottery and was so grateful God put these precious folks in my path.

She wrote their names and address on the envelope, and when I arrived at my mother's I sent them a thank you note to let them know we had arrived safely. We exchanged Christmas cards, as well as sending them the kids school pictures for years. I felt a strong bond with them and always felt they were sent from heaven. Who knows what might have happened if I had fallen asleep at the wheel that night if they hadn't flashed their headlights and scared me into being awake? After several years, I received a note from her daughter that told me they had both passed within just a few months apart after receiving my annual Christmas card. She told me in the letter that they had shared with her how they met me and the school pictures I sent them each year of the kids.

One would have a hard time convincing me that angels don't exist, as I met two of them on a desert road late one night and they most likely saved our lives.

Chapter 11
Returning to Casa Grande – A New Chapter in our Lives

Despite what my father and brothers had done in the past, I felt I could return home in Casa Grande to raise my children without too many issues. RC had past, Gary was in prison serving two life sentences and Joe, had married well, and living in Casa Grande and running what was then called The Arches with his father-in-law. If I worked hard and involved in the schools and community, everything would be all right. I would hopefully be judged on my own merits. I never in a million thoughts considered Gary escaping from prison again or Joe's connection to the Mexican Cartel, running drugs from Mexico and Larry's running a Chop Shop. Life is just full of surprises, especially with my brothers.

Upon getting close to Casa Grande, I was a bit confused as there were no freeways here when I left years ago, however I remember Florence Boulevard, so I thought if I got off this freeway there I would know where to go from there to find my mother's place. She lived on Kadota Avenue in a small one-bedroom duplex. Although she made me and the kids feel welcomed and safe, even the dogs, outside of course. I knew I had to get a place to live right away. Christmas was nearing and she had put up a little tree on a stand. The tiny Christmas tree was like going back in time for me, during the times our father was in prison, mother always went to the Christmas tree lot on Christmas eve and got the last of the tiny trees for us to decorate. She was proud to have it up and the kids enjoyed it, so that was all that was important. We were safe although I was scared to death about our future and how we would survive.

Growing up we never had much money, so we always had a small tree. Once I had my own home with kids, I always wanted a big tree, we even popped popcorn to string like in the movies, alternating with cranberries that always dried out before Christmas time and took on the look of raisins, but we always had fun making them. We stayed with mother till right after New Years', and I found us an apartment not far from her. I called Bekins to let them know when they could deliver my things after putting down a deposit. I knew I had to get a job and quickly as I was running low on money and had no resources except to work and earn more.

On January 3, 1975, I took the kids to school, and all dressed up I started downtown to apply for a job as a secretary for a law firm. I met all their qualifications and was excited about getting the position and kept telling myself "It was mine," the power of positive thinking and all. However right in front of the Police Department I had a flat tire and pulled into their parking spots to go inside and call someone to come and fix my tire. A new one wasn't in my budget, so it had to be repaired and last for a bit longer. I told myself "Don't let this affect your enthusiasm, you're going to get this job, this is just a bump in the road." After going inside, I walked up to a window that had bars but no security glass like there is now in so many Police Departments. There was what looked like a secretary, a dispatcher and a large, Hispanic male who was wearing sergeant stripes. He was friendly and asked if he could help me. He even walked out into the lobby and shook my hand, as it was obvious, he recognized me, although I couldn't say the same about him. I explained I'd had a flat out front and was wondering if I could use their phone to call someone, and he escorted me into an office. Immediately he smiled and said, "I know you; you are Lynda Tison." He extended his hand and said, "My name is Sgt. Gastelum." Nobody had called me that in a long, long time and I nodded and said "Yes, well I used to be, my name is Smith now."

He started quizzing me about not seeing me for years and I explained I had been married to a military man and had been gone for a long time but was back now with my three children and headed to apply for a job when I had the flat. He told me they had a dispatcher position open, and perhaps I'd like to apply for that. He said it paid $925 per month plus medical. Damn, that seemed like a good job, but would they hire a Tison? After all, everyone knew my father and brothers and knew they were career criminals, and I was sure this sergeant was no exception, yet he seemed genuine about offering me a job. He got me an application, asked me which car was mine and went out and changed my tire for me while I filled out the application, taking the damaged one in for repairs. I was impressed to say the least and a bit embarrassed that my spare probably wasn't the best, but at least it wasn't flat. I didn't really think they would hire me when the higher-ups found out my maiden name. I didn't take the application profoundly serious and even put "occasionally" when it asked for sex, meaning of course, male or female. It was years after I was hired before the chief's secretary caught it one day while updating her files. She thought it was funny, and I guess she never brought it to anyone else's attention, which was to my advantage.

I graciously thanked Sgt. Gastelum, gave him my application, and went on to the law office to apply for that position. I was saddened to see so many applicants in the office applying for the same position. I remained positive and knew I would find a job.

Early the next morning, I received a call from the Police Department asking if I was available for an interview that afternoon and immediately wished I had taken the application process a bit more seriously. I was interviewed by two sergeants, one of them being Sgt. Gastelum and the chief's secretary, with a couple other sergeants sitting in on the interview. They explained the job requirements and that there would be different shifts, to include day, swing, and midnight, and that the shifts rotated every three months. I assured them none would be a problem and that my mother would help me until I found a reliable babysitter. One of the sergeants told me right out, "We know your maiden name is Tison, and this is a concern to me. Are you in anyway like your brothers and do you have a relationship with them?" I assured him I was in no way like any of them and hadn't had any type of relationship with any of them in years and wasn't planning on starting. I also assured him I had a clean record, never being arrested for anything, had not even received a speeding ticket. I explained that my father and brothers had chosen their path in life, and I had chosen mine, and they were two different paths. By then I had two years of college under my belt and assured this inquisitive sergeant that I was going to continue with classes at Central Arizona College and work toward a degree, which I did. I also told him due to being a single parent, it would take a while, but it was my goal. He gave his approval, as did the other sergeants and the secretary, and I was to start the following day on swing shift.

I had no idea what O'Odham Tash was and just how many people were in town for it and how busy the cops were going to be. There was one radio dispatcher for not only the local police officers but Indian Police, DPS and others, all on the same frequency during this All-Indian Rodeo. No automation and sophisticated equipment, just one dispatcher, a secretary next to her that took incoming calls, and as I stood there watching, it looked like a total clusterfuck, and I had absolutely no idea what I was doing. Sgt. Gastelum sort of took me under his wing and gave me a list of codes that were to be used on the radio. I looked at him and ask him how long I would have to learn them. He looked at his watch and said, "Fifteen minutes." I desperately needed this job and didn't want to screw it up but knew it was virtually impossible for me to learn all these codes in fifteen minutes. When I finally was placed at the Dispatcher's desk, he patted me on the back and said, "Just do the best you can." There was a second frequency that we could speak regular English on, not codes, so Sgt. Gastelum activated the microphone and told all officers to switch over, which they did. He told them we had a new dispatcher who hadn't had time to learn the codes and to be patient and work with her. There were lots of *click clicks* to indicate they would ... I had absolutely no idea what I was in for.

As we received call after call, I would quickly look up the codes and felt I was doing as good a job as could be expected, considering my fifteen-minute training session. Oh yes and we had to write down such things as the officer's location when stopping a vehicle, their license number, address of house they were going into, etc. This all had to be done by hand on a sheet of paper, no typewriter, no computer, just a pen and paper with phones constantly ringing and trying to get officers where they needed to be or information to them. During this seasonal rodeo, the phone lines were ringing all at once, or so it seemed, and the secretary was rattled and couldn't take them all, so it became apparent that I needed to also take calls. Later in the evening, I took a call from a lady whose husband was beating her up, she managed to give me her address before the husband ripped the phone out of her hand and hung it up, but just as he did, I could hear her screaming and begging for help, "send someone quick please." Remembering my own personal history of physical abuse, I was compassionate for this woman and wanted to get officers to her as quickly as possible.

In my opinion, there was no time to look up a code and having personally experienced what this woman was living through, decided I was going to get her help as quickly as possible. I activated the microphone and said "There is one hell of a family fight going on at such and such address and the wife needs help immediately. I don't think anyone has a gun." That was one especially important question to ask the caller when there was an incident, but considering my lack of training, I didn't think to ask. Lt. Bain responded with "That will be a 415-F Dispatcher." I never forgot that code again, let me tell you, and knew the officers responding were probably laughing at me and wondering what kind of dumb ass they had hired. Shortly after that, I was removed from the radio and given another fifteen-minute training session about how important it was for officers to know if any weapons were involved. It surely made sense to me that I should have asked and probably asked everybody that called in after that "Does anyone have a weapon?" It was quite an experience, and I felt if I made it through O'Odham Tash I probably wasn't going to get fired.

After three months of working swing shift, I was rotated to graveyard shift, which was a bit difficult since I had three small children, but again desperately needed the job, so I never mentioned it at work. I found a lady who would sleep at my house and was able to take my lunch break at 5 a.m. so I could run home and make lunches for the boys to take to school and lay out their school clothes. My plan was to rush home as soon as I was relieved at 8 a.m., take the boys to school and DeAnna to day care so I could sleep a few hours. Since there was a debriefing at the end of each shift, this didn't work out so well for me and my schedule. I got my mother to drive the boys to school until I felt they were responsible enough to walk and had the lady staying overstay until I got home to take DeAnna to Day Care.

I had moved from the apartments to a brand-new home on Lehmberg in a nice neighborhood. It wasn't a fancy house, but for me it was new, and I was so proud, as I'd never lived in or even been in a brand-new home. I bought it on a contract from the developer and assured him I would never miss a payment of $239 per month. The kids needed a place to play outside, out of the sun, so I designed and built a porch over the patio area. I'd never built anything, but I bought a book that said, "How to Build a Patio If You Don't Know How." Sort of seemed like the book for me, and for $1.99 at the grocery checkout stand, I felt it was a good investment. I saved a little out of each check to buy the lumber and other supplies I would need and was finally ready to start my project. After spreading the ABC, I had bought, watered, and packed it like the book said, I was finally ready to have the concrete delivered on my day off. All three kids enjoyed wetting it down every night and dancing on it to pack it down like the book said. I was all ready to finish it out when the driver asked, "who is coming to help you finish this concrete out." I very confidently said, "I can do this, just lay it out for me." He assured me in a sarcastically voice that you lay bricks and cheap women, but you pour concrete. Well, I learned a valuable lesson that day about concrete and thankfully I wasn't married to this piece of shit man who drove the truck. For those who do concrete work for a living, I'm sure you wouldn't have thought it wasn't the best job and it got away from me quick. The concrete truck driver stood and watched with his hands on his hips and at no time offered to help me out. I kept telling myself, "I can do this." I've learned over the years that often my positive thinking kept my ass in trouble. Well, it for sure wasn't the best-looking patio in town, but the kids had a place to play out of the sun once I got the framing and roof up. The framing looked better than the concrete, but the kids didn't mind. I even let them put all their initials in the wet cement and some thirty years later, one of my sons called to say he was in the backyard for some reason and wanted me to come and look at the initials that were still there.

Standing in this backyard with him, my mind drifted back to those times which now seemed like a million years ago. It was also a reminder to me why my kids grew up with such confidence, knowing they could do anything they put their minds to because they had watched their mother take on projects that only a totally and complete insane single mother of three would take on, I had no choice, no one else to call and no one to depend on except myself. However, they didn't think of me as being totally and completely insane, they thought I was just smart and aggressive and looking back, I suppose that's what kept me going, the fact that they believed in me and trusted me for their guidance and direction.

Chapter 12
Working for Casa Grande Police Department and Ambulance

"Life" seemed to be moving along well with my new job at Casa Grande Police Department after relocating back here to start over with my children, even with the changing of shifts every three months. I knew I had to keep my distance from Joe who lived in Casa Grande at the time with his wife, just down the street from me on Manor Drive. I went out of my way to avoid him although he did stop by periodically, supposedly to see how I was doing. Joe always, and I do mean always, had ulterior motives, so my guard was always up with him.

He was running the Arches' Restaurant and Cocktail Lounge with his partner and father-in-law. His father-in-law was a city councilman and pretty much a big shot here in Casa Grande. However, when things went south with the business of The Arches and Joe got caught running drugs in his private plane, he of course, blamed Joe; after all Joe was a Tison, and he simply didn't know when he went into business with him, what he was getting into and didn't know he was running drugs. Hello! Joe ultimately built a beautiful home at the base of Casa Grande Mountain for cash, had his own landing strip and airplane, and was gone a lot at night. Who couldn't have figured this out? Of course, his family was enjoying the good life, so his father-in-law apparently just turned a blind eye and acted like he didn't know what's going on, even though some of the profits were going back into the business to be washed.

Going back a few years, Joe put Larry up to robbing a meat packing place in Casa Grande. Larry was a young boy and still in junior high. After getting caught, he told the police who put him up to it, but being upstanding citizens in town, Joe and his father-in-law denied knowing anything about it. Joe told the police that Larry had never been any good and wasn't surprised that he would do this. The two, with their families, enjoyed all the benefits from this robbery in backyard BBQs by the pool while Larry did eighteen months in Ft. Grant, a juvenile facility in the southeastern part of Arizona. Mother – like with Gary, Joe, and our father – dragged us down at least one Sunday a month to have a picnic with Larry and tell him God was looking out for him and that the Church women were all praying for him. He looked like he didn't care about the church people, but he sure enjoyed the homemade food we brought. We always had to make extra cookies so we could leave them for him. Larry had told my parents on the very first visit who had put him up to robbing that Meat Packing Co. and if the police would just check their freezers, they would find the meat and prove they had put him up to it. However, with my father, Joe was always the "Golden Boy" who did nothing wrong, and Joe and RC both threatened to kick Larry's ass if he ever said anything like that to anyone again. Larry did his eighteen months, and I was probably the only one who believed him, I already realized he wasn't any different than the other men in our family, I just knew he didn't rob that meat packing facility without Joe putting him up to it, telling him he and his father-in-law would protect him. Our father started early with them all, teaching them how to hotwire cars, steal, lie and con. I suppose nobody ever told our father that honesty pays in the end. Either nobody told him, or he just didn't get it or give a damn. That fast money just came far too easy for all of them, even knowing they would eventually end up in prison again.

***

Anyway, one night after my day shift at CGPD Joe stopped by while I was cooking dinner for my kids, in no uncertain terms told me he could put me to work tomorrow making big money and be home with my kids more. Joe always scared me, and nobody said no to him without consequences, much like Gary. However, I looked him in the eye and said "And who the hell takes care of my kids when I go to prison for working with you? I think not. I'll keep doing what I'm doing, and God will protect me." Not only did I get an earful but got cussed like never before and he kept telling me how stupid I was for not joining him in his business. He left, slamming the door, but his last words were "You stupid, ignorant bitch." I had sent the kids outside to play so they wouldn't hear all this, and after Joe left, I just stood at the patio door thinking about how blessed I was to be able to love and care for these precious little ones, and even felt blessed for the two jobs I needed to care for them. They were the ultimate joy of my heart and was what kept me going with little to no sleep and able to work two jobs, yet still found time to spend with them.

Years later, I contacted a friend of mine who was with the U.S. Marshall's Office to ascertain where Joe was after yet another arrest. He informed me he was in a federal prison in Tucson under an alias name. He obtained permission for me to visit him, as I needed to tell him our mother had been declared incompetent due to dementia which was later diagnosed as Alzheimer's. Despite whom and what he was, this was our mother, and I felt he deserved to know. I made the trip, and one of the first things he said to me was "I apologize for calling you stupid for working two jobs and barely making it years ago. You were the smart one and did it the right way, and here I am sitting in another federal prison, so I apologize." He also knew I drove a Cadillac and lived in a beautiful home. I was curious about how he knew so much about me, but I wasn't there for that and let it go. I explained to him what mother was going through and said with that last name, I needed to get her out of the county mental health facility and into a Desert Valley Nursing Home for better care. In the county facility, she was receiving undeniable poor care. I didn't know if it was because of who she was or their poor practice of taking care of older, ill patients. I found her more than once tied to a chair with dried feces all over her bottom and back side. It disturbed me more than anyone would ever know. I would shower her and try to comfort her although often she didn't know who I was, she often thought I worked for the care center. I would kindly and gently bring this to the attention of the staff nurse but was met with aggressiveness and an angry response of "We're understaffed, and she is tied to the chair for her own protection." Dear Lord! Either way, I knew I had to get her out of there and into a better facility. I was having tremendous difficulty, due to her last name, getting any sort of approval from the county to help with funding, although I was going to hire an attorney and continue trying.

I would go daily, arriving as soon as the County Facility in Florence for funding would open, sit for hours, and wait, hearing laughter and such from behind the door. I was asked to leave this funding office at lunch so they could close and come back at 1 pm, which I did. During the lunch hour I would go to the County facility where mother was, take her clean clothes, shower her, and make her as comfortable as I could. This went on for three days until the young receptionist followed me outside of Florence after 5:00 when they closed, flashed her lights, and wanted me to pull over to speak with me. She said "I have a deadbeat dad with two kids, and I really need this job, but I feel so badly for you. They are never going to see you or approve your mother for Desert Valley Care Center because of her last name." She went on to explain they all laughed behind closed doors about how this county had already spent too much money on the Tisons and they sure as hell weren't going to take care of the old lady. I was stunned, but I should have already figured it out after three days of waiting in their lobby. I promised this young girl nobody would ever know it came from her and would protect her job but that I had to relay this information to my attorney. She said she understood and said "I hope it all works out for you and your mom, but this office isn't going to do anything to help you. Good luck and God bless you." As I drove to the ranch, I had a mixture of anger and severe sadness and felt so hopeless and unable to protect my mother. However, being the persistent person I've always been, I knew I wasn't about to quit.

When I went to see Joe in the federal prison in Tucson, I said to him in no uncertain terms that he had always bragged about all the money he made running drugs, etc. and now I needed him to help our mother, not me. Although Joe always scared me, I felt somewhat safe with prison guards around, I mean what could he do to me there inside the visiting room? At this point I was married to Frank and he and I were prepared to pay for Desert Valley Care Center here in Casa Grande, but the cost was exorbitant, and I felt Joe needed to pay half, as he was as responsible as anyone for our mother losing her mind. Joe agreed, went to one of the Guards, got a pen and paper, and wrote down his attorney's name/number for me to contact. Well of course, I thought he was blowing smoke, but I stopped at the first pay phone after leaving the prison to call this attorney. He said Joe had called and told him I would be contacting him. He asked for my address, and I explained I wanted no part of Joe's drug money but once I moved mother into this facility then he could send checks directly to the nursing home, which to my surprise, he did. He paid half; we paid the other half until a few months later when I was able to get her under a county program to pick up some of the cost. I was told explicitly by yet another county employee that this county had spent enough money on the Tison family and wasn't going to take care of the old lady. Wow! I was blown away again even the second time I heard it, but after my attorney and I went in like gangbusters to the County Manager's Office, citing rules, regulations and statues and showed him how mother met all of their guidelines, he clearly and rather abruptly said, "If you don't approve Mrs. Tison for care today, this Tison standing next to me will own this fucking county and your ass." Within two hours, it was done. However, when we first walked in, my attorney did not introduce me, he got right down to business. However, this manager, being the suck up he was tried to make small talk to this well-known and respected attorney, asking him how the family was doing, etc. There was no response to his questions, only the statement above. Honestly, I have to say I found it rather entertaining to watch him crawl after he got his ass handed to him, citing the rules, regulations, and such.

Several years later I was sponsoring a fundraising event for foster children and this manager came as the County of Pinal had purchased $2,000 worth of tickets at $100 each to support the programs PCCI offered. He quickly figured out I was in charge and came up offering his extended hand to me to introduce himself. I smiled graciously, thanking him for coming even though he hadn't paid for the ticket himself, the County had, shook his hand and said "actually we have met, several years ago, I was in your office about county funding for my mother. My name is Lynda Tison." His expression was priceless.

***

Going back to the federal prison visit with Joe to let him know our mother had been declared incompetent, he had asked me about mother's pearls. Wow! Seriously!? I knew she had a set of pearls and loved to wear them for special occasions, but it never dawned on me that they might be real pearls. I told Joe sitting in that visiting room that mother had given them to me a few years ago and ask me to "Do what was right with them when I'm gone," still believing that they were just something she loved dearly. I put them in my safe deposit box at the bank and never thought too much more about them until Joe asked, but quickly realizing they had monetary value since he had asked me about them. I questioned him about them, and he chuckled and said, "They were on bonus on a job RC, and I did years ago, and RC wanted to give them to mother." *Holy cow* was the only thing that came to mind, although my little mind was racing, knowing mother would have never treasured them if she had known they had been stolen; she only held them dear because RC had given them to her. He suggested I sell them, saying they would probably more than pay for Desert Valley Care Center for mother for years to come. For me, this was out of the question, although not really knowing what to do with them now or where they had come from, as he wouldn't tell me the details of how he and RC had acquired them although I continually asked. My thoughts were that they should be returned to the family they were stolen from, but Joe would not say.

When mother died in 1993, I woke up early on Saturday morning of her funeral with the reminder what she had told me years prior: "Do what you think is right with the pearls when I'm gone," not even knowing at the time she gave them to me that they were real pearls.

Mother passed in 1993 after a six-year battle with Alzheimer's, ultimately dying of a stroke. I placed her placed in Desert Valley Care Center but saw her daily until her death. I would go by the nursing home with an Ice Cream Sundae each night on my way home and read her the Bible scriptures that she so loved. Also eating lunch with her often in the dining room. She often introduced me as "her friend." As sad as it was, I didn't take it personal, she was suffering from Alzheimer's. She didn't know me but I it was obvious she enjoyed having me there. When I was out of town, I had a schedule set up for my kids to visit her, take clean clothes and make sure she was alright and report to me via phone. She was so helpless and frail, and had such a dysfunctional life, I felt the least I could do, at this stage of her life, was to make her as comfortable and content as possible.

I called Jere the morning after she passed, he was our friend and the manager at a local bank in Casa Grande, and he of course, offered his condolences. I asked him if I could obtain something out of my safe deposit box to bury with my mother. He explained, even as president of the bank, he had to have two people to open after hours but that he would take care of it and call me back, which he did within a couple of hours. I met him in the bank, got the pearls, and took them to the funeral home asking the owner if they would please put them on my mother, as they were hers, and I felt she should wear them to heaven since she loved them so much. I knew I was going to get some flack at least from one sister, and I did. However, I did what I thought was right at the time, which is what mother had asked me to do. Years later when my daughter married, I looked at her in her beautiful wedding dress and wished she were able to wear the pearls since they meant so much to mother, but it was obviously too late. With four girls in our family and several nieces, I knew it was going to create havoc for us all ... so, I did what I thought was right and had mother buried with them around her neck.

***

Going back a few years to working at the police department, with the help of my mother and a sitter to sleep at the house while I worked nights, I felt safe from abuse and happy with my kids. Unfortunately, though, as the kids grew and active in school, their needs got greater, and the money simply wasn't enough, so I took on a second job.

While as a military dependent, living in such isolated places in Germany, the military had provided lots of medical training so we could care for our children in non-emergency situations when there was no hospital available in some of the isolated villages, we were stationed in. The information/training I was gaining there was interesting and since I wasn't working while living in Europe decided I'd put that time to good use and be able to care for the kids if something happened. They also provided day care for the kids, and I got to eat in the mess hall, which I thought was fairly good food, while the kids ate at the military day care center. Both boys loved being at the day care with all the toys and socialization of other kids as we were isolated generally all the time .... it was a win-win for all. It all seemed to make sense and since I enjoyed it so much, I continued past the first-aid stage and just kept attending. At some point one of the instructors informed me I had earned a paramedic status. Wow, I wasn't even sure what that meant, but it sure came in handy years later when I needed that second job.

Looking for a second job, I was hired by Southwest Ambulance Co. with the understanding that my primary job was with the Casa Grande Police Department and that I was a single parent with three children. Considering I was paramedic status, I got paid $10 per hour, unlike EMTs who were paid $8. I also attended the Department of Safety

Driving School, offered by Arizona Highway Patrol, so I was also able to operate the ambulance, which also contributed to even higher pay. I had to work my shifts in between my primary job and kids, but it seemed to be working for me, and I kept telling myself "Who needs sleep" and the money was a life changer for me. I was able to buy my kids those extra little items that meant so much to them, like sports equipment, clothing, baseball gloves and such. My boss felt they had made a good decision in hiring me even though I had stipulations such as a full-time job and three small children. Al Ortega was my supervisor with Southwest and just a good guy. I think he felt sorry for me, but also appreciated my knowledge and being on board as a responsible medic. I always noticed more hours on my timecard each week than I had put in. He knew I knew, but it was never spoken of. Many years later, he and his wife bought a home from me, and I was able to Pay It Forward to him. Once again, it wasn't spoken of, however we both knew, and he gave me a hug and said, "God bless you." I assured him he already had when I worked for him, as those few extra hours he put on my timecard meant the difference in whether we ate meat with our meals and occasionally night out for me and the kids at Taco Bell and Dairy Queen. One of our favorite treats was to get banana splits from Dairy Queen; we'd walk across the street to Peart Park, sit in the grass, and pig out on ice cream. After that, we would swing for what felt like hours. It was good, quality time with my kids despite the fact I worked so many hours and wasn't always with them.

Once on a graveyard shift about 3 a.m., I laid my head on the desk and went sound asleep. The radio was quiet, and

my officers were probably also sleeping out there somewhere. Chief Cozad walked in and was extremely upset
with me and said to be in his office at eight in the morning.
I was far more concerned about how this was going to
disrupt my schedule with the kids and my other job than
how much trouble I was in. He was notorious for looking
over his glasses when he spoke, he was just a scary man, at
least to those who worked for him and of course, he was
our boss – the chief of police. I was more than shocked
when he told me he never wanted to hire me anyway because of my criminal family, but Sgt. Gastelum and Lt. Hall
had asked him to give me a shot. By now, I had worked
there for quite a while and had been an exemplary employee. For the life of me, I couldn't figure out what falling
asleep on the job and my bad ass father and brothers had
to do with this, but he was the chief, and I just shook my
head yes and said, "I understand, sir." He asked me what I
had to say in my defense and after apologizing, I said, "Sir, I
work two jobs and have three kids; if I didn't sleep on the
job, I wouldn't get any sleep at all." I guessed that wasn't
what he wanted to hear and gave me three days off without
pay. I apologized again and doubled up on hours for my ambulance job.

When I returned to duty, I was given strict instructions
that there would be no more sleeping on the job and was
considered probationary for three months. My medical
insurance for me and the kids was tied to this job, so I
surely couldn't afford to lose it.

Sgt. Davis informed me the first night back that I would
be relieved for a couple of hours to train for searching and
securing female inmates as they were brought in. In my

simple mind, I was trying to determine if this was a promotion or punishment for falling asleep on the job. But I did exactly as I was told. As luck would have it, one of the officers brought in two extremely drunk Native American females, and I was relieved from the radio room to start training. Sgt. Davis was a good man and a good cop that I had known most of my life, but he was very direct and to the point. He explained about search and said once the inmate was against the wall to ask them to spread their legs. If they didn't, kick them apart but in no way bend down to move their legs as I would be putting myself in a situation where I could get hurt. Well that just seemed so inhuman to me so once I had these huge, drunk, Native American inmates hands up against the wall I asked her nicely to spread her legs so they could be searched. She told me to fuck myself and refused to do it. At first, I had asked nice, then louder, and direct, almost screaming at her, as if I could scare her into doing what I had asked. This woman must have been around 350 pounds, extremely drunk and aggressive, and I thought I was going to scare her!? Not in this lifetime! I was about 105 pounds, and she obviously knew I couldn't take her down. Although growing up with the Tison boys, I learned to fight long before I learned to read and write; I'd fight for something as simple as the last biscuit on the table at breakfast. For a skinny, lightweight kid, I was tough but only because I had to be to survive my childhood. At this time, standing in the jail I felt compassion and simply didn't want to kick her legs apart remembering how horrible it was for me as a kid to get knocked around and beat on.

Standing nearby watching, Sgt. Davis, said, "You know

what to do," never interfering or making any attempt to move toward me or the inmates, however I still felt it was inhuman and he was just being mean. I bent down to move her legs apart and when I did, her right arm came off the wall, and she hit me with full force, breaking my nose. Blood everywhere and, great pain, I then kicked her legs apart as Sgt. Davis had told me to do in the beginning. After I secured both inmates with blood dripping down my face and onto my uniform and floor, Sgt. Davis then said, "You should get medical treatment." Really!? I called the fire dept., and two medics came and took me to the emergency room.

I insisted they take me back to work because after all, it was my first night back after suspension, and I wanted to finish my shift and try to impress my Sgt., and mainly the chief.

Of course, Chief Cozad already knew of the incident by being briefed in the squad room by our shift commander. He walked into the radio room at 7:30 a.m. and you can only imagine my surprise when he said, "Trouble just seems to follow you and your family doesn't it?" I was overwhelmed by his lack of concern and/or compassion for me and hatred for my family, the latter part I understood but if he didn't want me there, he should have fired me not humiliate me in front of the entire squad and treat me differently from the others. It was a life-changing, emotional moment for me as I realized once again that the world was a mean, cruel place and I better toughen up even more if I wanted to survive. Growing up with that horrible, career criminal father and bad ass brothers of mine, I should have already known this without a doubt. However, I thought as a normal, good-hearted, honest, hard-working, functioning adult, people would be better to me. However, even though some were mean and cruel just because of whom I was related to, I never wanted to lose my compassion for others having lived through so much growing up and now having to deal with this Tison bullshit as an adult. Many, many times I asked myself why I ever came back to this town, but at that point in my life, I couldn't afford to move, so I decided to suck it up, stay on the straight and narrow, raise my kids and move forward. Little did I know that Gary would escape from prison in 1978, kill innocent people, causing the biggest man hunt in history in the Southwest and that it would get 100% worse. It's now been forty years plus, and it still surfaces when you least expect it to. I expect it will never, ever go away, but I continued the straight and narrow, never having to look over my shoulders and taught my kids, as my mother had said to me, "You're not guilty by relationship" although we've paid a horrendous price for all they have done in their past.

As if it weren't enough to be in pain from getting the crap knocked out of me by that big Indian woman in the jail, I looked worse than some of the patients we picked up in the ambulance with my bandages, swollen face, and blackened eyes. My partner in the ambulance was a medical intern at the local hospital and worked the ambulance for additional money. When I showed up for my shift, he looked at me and said, "Shit I've sent people to the mortuary looking better than you, what the hell happened?" I explained my incident at the jail, and he gave me a big hug and said, "You're tough; I think I would have quit." Of course, when patients looked at me with surprise when we showed up at a scene with a gurney, I would laugh with them and say the adage about

"You should see the other guy." What the hell is girl supposed to do or say? I needed both jobs.

I continued to keep my distance from Joe and Larry and, of course, Gary was in and out of prison his entire adult life, so I didn't have to worry about him much. However, after getting off a swing shift one night, Joe was waiting for me at my house. He had told the babysitter he needed to talk to me when I got there and that we'd go out on the patio for privacy but asked her to stay, as we would be leaving soon after. He paid her for the week with a bonus, so of course she was willing to wait. He was accustomed to getting what he wanted even if it meant paying for it, and my babysitter was no exception. Apparently within the 20-30 minutes he waited for me, they became great friends and were laughing and joking when I walked in. Joe had a great personality, was a classy looking man, and was well liked .... until you realized what he was capable of.

I got a real sick feeling in the pit of my stomach because I knew if he were there, especially at that time of night, something was not good. We went out on the patio, and he explained to me that a friend of his had been shot and I needed to go with him to patch him up. I said, "Absolutely not"! I reminded him that my life was different from his and I wanted nothing to do with this situation. He looked at me with cold dark eyes and said, "I wasn't asking, grab your medical bag." He took me to his truck in the front with a firm grip on my arm, as though he expected me to run, and we went to a truck stop area at Interstate 10 and Sunland Gin Road. He had a mobile home behind it, and anytime I passed by, I couldn't help always wonder what the hell was going on in there, knowing Joe.

When we got inside, he took me into the bedroom area, and there was a man lying on the bed bleeding badly from the shoulder. Joe said, "Fix him." Holy shit, this guy had been shot, and the bullet went in one side and out the other of his shoulder. I explained he needed a doctor, not a paramedic. He grabbed my arm and said, "Fix him." I was so scared on so many levels I can even imagine where to begin but the thought that most entered my mind was my children and that I was in a really bad situation, surrounded by some bad guys. It looked like they had robbed a pharm-acy from all the medical supplies they had, and I did what I could but kept insisting that he needed a doctor, but my re-quest continued to fall on deaf ears. There were other men in the living room area, and they were all whispering, and I could have cared less about what. I just wanted to get the hell out of there.

After what seemed like hours, I walked into the living room and told Joe that his friend was patched up as good as it was going to get and reminded him again, he needed a doctor. I asked Joe to go outside with me and told him I would have to report this because I had taken an oath to report any gunshot wounds. He assured me he understood and asked if I would please just wait till tomorrow after-noon and I realized again, he wasn't asking, he was telling me. I agreed under duress, and some guy I'd not seen before came outside and Joe said for him to take me home.

Once home, after a hot shower, I laid in bed crying and wondering what the hell they had done to get this guy shot, but truth is, I didn't care. I was just pissed that he had involved me. I knew I had to wait until the following day to report because nobody, including me, wanted the wrath of

Joe Tison.

When I arrived at work the following morning, the entire department was scurrying around and talking about Paul Stein being shot and killed, they also were talking about how he got off at least one shot, so the attacker had to be injured. The sickening realization was this is the guy Joe had made me patch up.

I received a call from Joe at the Police Department that day, and he said to meet him at the Arches Bar when I got off work. Walking in there around 4:30, my hands were shaking, and I kept thinking I was going to throw up. But whatever happened, I knew I was going to go back to the police department and report that gunshot wound to Sgt. Stanford, my shift commander.

As I waited about thirty minutes, a guy whom I'd never seen before walked up and asked if I was Lynda, Joe's sister. When I said yes, he suggested we move to a table away from the bar and out of earshot of anyone else. He said, "Joe couldn't make it, but he sent me. You will not report that gunshot wound. You were never there and none of this happened, do you understand?" Of course, being the person I am, I explained to him I didn't have a choice, that I had taken an oath to report such things and it was my duty to do so. He ordered a drink and looked me directly in the eyes when he said to me "DeAnna is a pretty little girl, and I'd hate to see her face scarred up, and this is what will happen if you open your fucking mouth to anyone about what you saw or you did." I was horrified and decided I would call Joe. This bad guy who I didn't know, assured me that Joe had gone out of state and that I would not be able to contact him now or in the future and to not even try, as it would not be in my best interest, or my daughter's best interest. At that point I did have to throw up and ran to the lady's room. I kept washing my face afterwards trying to believe this was all a bad dream and I'd wake up and it would be gone. Unfortunately, it wasn't a dream, and everything I knew about my brother was that if I said anything to anyone, the consequences would be devastating. I went back out and assured this bad guy that I would say nothing to anyone, and I left. I didn't take any calls for the ambulance that night. I had hot dogs and chips for the kids and took them to Dairy Queen afterwards. Their laughter and playfulness were so simple and pure, and they trusted me to protect them. That night I had all three of them sleep in the bed with me, and as I watched them sleep, I prayed for God to protect and keep them safe from all harm.

For months, I couldn't look Sgt. Stanford or anyone else in the eyes at the Police Department as they all worked so diligently for the killer of Paul Stein. At least now, I knew what happened to the guy I had to patch up who had been shot. Paul Stein, who owned the Silver Bullet on Pinal Avenue, as well as other places of business, had a reputation of always having a gun nearby, and when they broke into his house, he obviously shot one of them. Unfortunately, they killed Paul. His wife was conveniently out of town when this happened, and as it turned out, she and Joe were good friends. I learned later that the two of them went to Hawaii shortly after Paul's death. As usual with Joe, I never mentioned what I had learned to anyone out of sheer fear of retaliation from him. I've never speculated on this because nobody will ever know the truth. However, Paul's wife, Francie, and I became friends years later through a couple of local organizations we were both involved in, and I always wanted to ask her about her friendship and the trips she took with my brother Joe but never did. Over our years of friendship, she periodically mentioned what a horrible life she had with Paul, and I got the feeling she was trying to tell me something without speaking the words ... that she had him killed. I always thought Joe had told her I was the one who patched up Paul's killer but most likely didn't mention how he made me do it or the threats that came afterwards to hurt my daughter if I came forward. I always thought Francie was subtly trying to justify her friendship with the man who was instrumental in killing her husband. I only responded to her that I was sorry she had such an awful life for so many years with her husband, yet in my heart knew it was best to let a sleeping dog lie. When she passed years later, some of our friends and I were in Jamaica at a resort. Having dinner, we all made a toast to her as she had died the day before we left and talk-ed about what a great lady, she was .... yet in the back of my mind, I always wondered if she and Joe had not conspired to kill her husband, Paul.

Months and months went by, and Paul's killer(s) were never found, and I always felt I could have trusted Sgt. Stanford as he was a good man, but I was so afraid of what Joe or his thugs would do to my daughter, so I lived with it for a long, long time, feeling guilty and ashamed.

One night on graveyard shift this strangely attractive man walked up to the dispatch's window about 3 a.m. and started chatting. He introduced himself as Jim Martin and said he was an undercover agent for DPS. I honestly thought he was just killing time, and I was bored, so we talked for a while. He then asked if I could take a break and have some breakfast with him. I told him I go home at 5 a.m. on my lunch break and prepare lunches for my kids but could go the squad room and have a cup of coffee, which we did. He was kind and gentle, with kind eyes, and when he spoke to me, he looked directly into my eyes. I worked all the time and took care of my kids, so I had no social life for years, so I must be honest saying I was excited about the attention he was giving me and that he kept telling me how pretty I was. Little did I know at the time, his undercover work involved my brother Joe for transportation of drugs from Mexico into the United States with his private plane. I suppose he thought since we were brother and sister, I knew something about his business, however I knew nothing and anytime his name came up, I changed the subject.

Jim came back several times and once asked me if I would go out with him. I was flattered but explained I didn't have time for dating. He suggested we at least go for breakfast on a Saturday or Sunday morning when I didn't have to rush home on my lunch break and make lunches for the kids. I agreed, and we went to a local restaurant for breakfast about 4 a.m. He told me he was attracted to me, that he was married but legally separated and was going to get a divorce. I learned later that none of this was true. Except for my late husband Frank, I had a history of picking the wrong men, and Jim was no exception, but I surely didn't know that at the time. All I knew was that my heart would race when he walked into a room, and I loved that he seemed to care so much for me. One Saturday morning when we were having breakfast, he took a pair of beautiful earrings out of his pocket and gave them to me. He said he thought about me when he saw them in the store. Our relationship grew over the next few months, and I felt like a woman again after so many years of not having anyone in my life.

Once at my house, he outright asked me if I knew anything about Joe's airplane and/or his drug business. I explained to him I didn't, didn't want to, and had nothing to do with my brothers, that they had chosen their path in life, and I had chosen mine and we were nothing alike. In my heart, I kept thinking this might have something to do with the guy who had been shot and perhaps he was leading up to that, as I had never breathed a word of that to anyone out of fear. I assured him I knew nothing and if I did, I wouldn't say anything because he didn't understand about Joe, and nobody wanted his wrath. Little did I know he knew more about Joe than anyone. He had been investigating him and his drug business for more than a year. I assumed that is why he got involved with me, thinking I could help him put Joe away. However, I knew nothing and always shied away from my brothers and especially after the gunshot incident. Unfortunately for Jim, he fell in love with me and went from apparently trying to use me for information to trying to protect me.

I had worked on the ambulance during the daytime that day, making two runs to Phoenix while the boys were in school and DeAnna at daycare, and was preparing to go on swing shift at the police department. The babysitter had arrived, dinner was on the stove and the kids were playing games at the table. Jim showed up, sat with the kids for a while, and they laughed, and he told them he needed to talk to their mom privately for a bit. They didn't mind that we went out on the patio to talk, DeAnna even gave Jim a hug before he went out, he had formed a strong relationship with my children. He had a strange look on his face when she gave him the hug, and I knew this wasn't going to be good. I assumed he was there to break up with me, perhaps even going back with his wife. Wow was I in for the shock of a lifetime!

He took my hands and said, "You knew from the beginning that I was an Undercover Agent for DPS, so I didn't lie to you about that. What I didn't tell you was that I have been investigating your brother Joe for over a year. When I first got involved with you, it was to hopefully obtain something from you that might help me put him away. Although I soon realized you didn't associate with him or know anything about his business. Also, I am not separated or getting a divorce, I have been with my wife all this time. I have fallen in love with you and will divorce my wife once this thing is over with your brother; hopefully, we can be together.

However, tonight I need you to call in sick because I'm going to be arresting Joe, and I don't want you in the building when I bring him in; you would have to process the paperwork, and it would just be better if you weren't there. I'm risking everything by telling you this, as you could call him and give him a heads up. I don't believe you would put me in the type of danger. We both know your brother is a dangerous man."

That familiar fear of wanting to throw up returned, and I excused myself and went into the bathroom. After throwing up, as I had done so many times over the years of incidents with my father and brothers, I sat in there for a while until he knocked on the door and asked to come in. He realized the pain I was in and obviously the hurt I was again experiencing after being told all this. He went to hug me, and I shrugged away from him, not wanting him anywhere near me. I yelled at him to get the fuck out of my house, and my life and to never attempt to contact me again.

Lord have mercy …. my little world just fell apart again, and all I could do was to look at him thinking "What an asshole." I promised to call in sick but that I wanted nothing else to do with him; it was obvious to me that he was a liar, deceitful and was probably lying about loving me so I would keep my mouth shut and not damage his investigation or prosecution of Joe if anyone found out about our involvement. I asked him to leave, called in sick, and the kids and I went to Dairy Queen and then to the park to swing. I couldn't believe what had just happened, but since I had a complete night off, I decided to spend it with my kids, as none of this was their fault and they deserved better.

***

Joe, my middle brother, probably had more opportunities that any human being I'd ever knew but managed to turn each one into an adventure of making fast money. He married a local city councilman and businessman's daughter. He didn't want his daughter to marry Joe and did everything in his power to prevent it. When he found out they had eloped, he contacted the police, used his contacts within the city, and had them picked up and detained in Wickenburg on their way to Las Vegas. After arriving to pick up his daughter at the county jail, she told him she loved him and would run away with him again as soon as she could.

Knowing his advice was falling on deaf ears to his daughter, knowing his daughter was going to go through with this marriage with or without his blessings, he decided to give his consent and got Joe out of jail. They had their wedding in Casa Grande; of course, none of us were invited because we weren't part of their social circle and would have been an embarrassment to Joe. Even as a young girl, I couldn't help but think "Wow, she has absolutely no idea of what she is getting into. Her life is going to be hell, as was ours, just living in the same house with them." They had two children, and her life was full of tragedy and disappointment, and, of course, courtrooms and prisons until she finally got out of the marriage and away from Joe.

As I learned later in life, his new father-in-law had profited from Joe's criminal activities and had one hell of a good "fall guy" due to Joe's reputation and history. However, due to the front Joe now had co-owning/operating The Arches, a local restaurant and bar, with his new father-in-law, my brother also was able to make lots of money, and built a beautiful, expensive home near Casa Grande Mountain for cash. They drove expensive vehicles, had a nice boat, ski trips, and lived a good life. His wife couldn't pretend she didn't know where the money was coming from and turned a blind eye when planes landed nearby at night and security around their house included men with large automatic rifles. They eventually bought a small gas station where Love's Truck Stop on Sunland Gin Road now sits, and anybody with half a brain would have known it didn't and couldn't possibly generate the kind of money they had become used to. I learned he had built a runway near his house and could take off and land a plane in the night without lights, always staying under the radar. I'd heard rumors

Joe was an ace pilot and running drugs from Mexico. As always, I kept my distance from him and his cohort that hung around the gas station and his home. I didn't want any part of this. I worked for CGPD and an am-bulance company and didn't need Joe's kind of problems, was simply attempting to build a life for my children and me. Years later, as part of a plea agreement, Joe told law enforcement he had stolen a grader and other heavy equipment from the City of Casa Grande to build his landing strip and where it was buried, near his property. No surprise when they dug it up and of course, again, front page news and more shame for our family. As part of Joe's plea agreement, they also wanted to know who the medic was that treated the gunshot wounds. He told them I did but didn't bother to tell them how I was picked up in the middle of the night to do this or that one of his thugs threatened to cut up my daughter's face. I spent hours trying to explain and was so apologetic to Sgt. Stanford that I had known all along who killed Paul Stein, when he and his detectives were busting their asses to solve this crime but was unable to tell him due to fear. He asked if I trusted him and of course I did, but my fear of Joe was greater, and he knew and understood that. Needless to say, I lost my job at the police department and the ambulance company as well, as I hadn't reported the gunshot wound I was forced to treat.

Chapter 13
Donnie Joe and the Escape

Donnie Joe was Gary and Dorothy's oldest son. He was intelligent, quick-witted, and wanted more out of his life than his father or brothers. He finished high school while working at Pizza Hut. He would often talk to his co-workers and friends about attending Central Arizona College (CAC) and then going onto Northern Arizona University. He would come by my house periodically and play ball with my boys, and we often talked about his future, as he did not want to take the path his father and uncles had. I had shared with him some – though not much, of my dysfunctional childhood and assured him that his dreams were possible for him to accomplish his goals if he really wanted it. It would be difficult, but I had done it and so could he with the right attitude and desire. I once told him that I was the first of my parents' seven children who graduated high school, the first one to ever go to college despite all I had to endure to do this, but I wanted him to know it was possible and would be easier for him if he just put his mind to it, and with determination went for it, not letting anyone or anything get into his way, especially his father. I assured him he did not have to grow up like his father, and although he loved his brothers, he knew they were never going to amount to anything except fixing up old cars and talking about outrunning police cars. He often told me how it irritated him when they talked tough like their father. He was just a good kid and as he got older, he no longer wanted those weekly visits to the prison to visit his father, despite the pressure from his mother.

I picked up some brochures from the military recruiting office and gave them to Donnie, talking to him about a VA sponsorship to college if he served a certain amount of time in the military. Nobody had ever explained to him how military service could benefit you for college. He said he once asked his dad, who told him it was a crock and not to bother. His dad had seriously discouraged his joining the Marines; in retrospect I'm sure it's because he needed him for his next planned escape. Donnie Joe joined the Marines as soon as he finished high school. I was extremely proud of him, as he was so determined not to end up like his father. He wanted so much out of life, not like his father, uncles, and grandfather, and was grateful that I had providing him information on college, and financial assistance through the VA that could help him obtain these goals, hopefully ultimately change his life.

After the Marines, he started taking classes at CAC. He had chosen criminal administration as his major and was so enjoying moving forward with his life. During his second year at CAC, he started coming around less and seemed despondent. I knew something was terribly wrong. All three boys were afraid of Gary, so he never broke confidence, not even with me about Gary's plans to escape. It was consistently drilled into the boy's heads that they could trust no one, except each other. He knew that if he told me, I would take the information to the officials and they would put Gary back in maximum security, in a much more secure place than where they had allowed him to be in the minimum-security complex.

I learned later that he wanted nothing to do with the escape and had desperately tried to get his brothers to not be involved. Ultimately his own mother, Dorothy, told me after Donnie's funeral that he only agreed to help on Saturday morning before the escape, to try to keep his brothers safe, not realizing what a narcissistic, sociopath his father really was, and his plans to kill everyone that got in his way. She did admit, though, that she had put a tremendous amount of pressure on him. I looked directly into her eyes standing on the front porch of her mother's house and asked how she could put her sons in this situation, knowing the dangers and Gary's inability or even concern to care for himself, much less his sons. I even went so far as to tell her I knew she had sent Donnie Joe and Ricky to my house to take me that Saturday prior to the escape to interpret the codes on the radios they intended to take during the escape and let her know she would have destroyed four more lives .... mine and my children's as I, too, either would have ended up in prison or Gary would have killed me, and that she had to know that. I reminded her that I was protected by Guardian Angels of God, and they couldn't take me due to Martha and her kids being at my place. Once again, God protected me and my children.

Her teary eyes dropped to the ground after I said all that was on my heart, and she responded with, "You don't think I haven't thought of that a million times since they blew my son's head off at the roadblock?" I just continued to look at her, and bitterly said "a bit late now, you buried one son today, the other two will spend the rest of their lives in prison." I walked away and never wanted to see her again.

Gary, Donnie Joe's brothers and his own mother had him convinced they would go straight to Mexico and live happily ever after, like a real family as they had been told. Unlike the Sunday visits at the prison, as the boys had been forced to do for far too many years. Donnie Joe once told me that while serving in the Marines, he was always thankful for Sundays and not having to go to the prison with his mother and brothers. He had shared with me how he detested going there as he got older and always thought "If they were all so smart, why were they all were locked up," referring to Gary, Joe, Larry, and our father. He said Sundays became his favorite day of the week, even if he was on military duty. After the military, during the time Donnie Joe was attending CAC, and working, he was missing those Sunday visits telling his mother he had homework since he worked all week as well. She bought it for a while, but as he told me, she continued to put pressure on him to go with her and the other two boys to the prison.

The Trustee Annex where Gary was housed was previously a female facility but was converted to a minimum-security facility area for male prisoners in 1976. No walls, only cyclone fencing lined with trees, grass and flowers maintained by the prisoners. It was a privilege to prisoners to be housed in this area and had to be earned and was a surprise to many, including many of the prison officials and guards when the warden had approved Gary for transfer, with his history of escapes and his knowledge of Gary's violence. However, Gary worked hard at getting himself reassigned there to plan his next escape, as it appeared so much easier than from inside the walls. As the editor of the prison newspaper and the constant praising of the warden allowed him special privileges, being reassigned was the most valuable one to him.

Joe had gotten Ricky and Raymond that Lincoln and guns for the escape early in 1978 but started having second thoughts about the risk he had taken, although he openly professed Gary couldn't get out of a paper bag, much less plan a successful escape. So, in November 1977 Joe informed Narcotics Division, once he knew they were onto him and his drug trafficking, that Gary was planning an escape in the spring of 1978. I suppose he made some sort of a plea agreement, however, continued with his trafficking only with more caution that before, leading the Narcotic personnel to think he had gone straight after giving him a break. He learned later that they continued to monitor him and ultimately, they arrested him again. The warden and other officials now knew of Gary's escape plans and acted by placing Gary back into maximum security. His escape plans were only postponed until he could maneuver himself with good behaviors and praise for the Warden and get back into minimum security. His plan only took a few months. Surprise, surprise – he was transferred back and vowed to kill Joe when he escaped for ratting him out.

***

The night before the escape, my kids and I were trying to decide what to make for dinner and whether we'd BBQ hamburgers or get pizza. We were living in Hacienda de Kadota apartments after dear brother Joe got me fired from the police department and my ambulance job. I lost my home after losing both my jobs. My brother-in-law was out of town so my sister, Martha dropped by with her kids, just hanging out. We talked about dinner and decided to grill some hamburgers. It was unusual for her to come by so late with the kids as they were usually home by that time of day. We didn't see each other all that often as they lived in Maricopa and I was busy making a living for my kids and I, working a lot of hours. When I did have free time, we normally spent it at the swimming pool. I would lay on a raft and listen to hours of Marko Polo. As we learned later, how God had protected me by her being there with her children.

As we started preparing to make hamburgers while the kids were watching TV in the living room and playing some sort of board game, there was a knock at the door. It was Donnie Joe and his brother, Ricky, the night before the escape. It wasn't unusual for Donnie Joe to stop by, as I had a relationship with him, and he often told me I inspired him to set goals and find a path unlike his father and uncles. Although extremely unusual for Ricky as I don't ever remember him ever being in my home, by his or my own choice. He and his brother, Raymond boasted often about the cops and how their cars could outrun any cop car and basically thought they were smarter than officers. Having grown up in a home where criminal activities were a daily part of our lives, so it seems with R.C. and my brothers, I was never impressed with this sort of talk and didn't care to be around them which was only at family funerals, weddings, and such.

Ricky kept asking me about working at the police department as a dispatcher, asking such things as how long it took me to learn all those codes used on the radio, did I by any chance still have a copy of them, etc., he said he thought it would be fun to know them. I immediately thought that his line of questions was rather odd. I told him I didn't remember how long it took to learn them all and I would still have that good job and my home, if good old Uncle Joe hadn't gotten me fired. After being fired from the police department and Southwest Ambulance due to Joe, I lost my home in foreclosure, forcing my kids and I to live in this small apartment. By then, I was getting a bit irritated and concerned, as was Martha. We kept looking at each other as if to say, "What do they want?" My gut was telling me that nothing about this visit was right; something was way off, but it wasn't registering with me.

They both appeared to be extremely agitated and nervous about something and kept trying to make small talk, but Ricky kept taking the conversation back to the police radio and codes. Ricky at one point asked if he could use the phone in my bedroom to call his mother; of course, I said all right, never guessing he was calling her to tell her that their plan was not working out. Ricky even went so far as to ask Martha if she was staying the night or was leaving after dinner. Martha said she thought they might just stay the night, and that probably saved my life. They left shortly after that. Donnie Joe kept hugging Martha and I, telling us how good it was to see us both and that he loved us. Little did we know then, that would be the last time we ever saw him.

As we learned after the escape, they had taken radios with them from the prison, radios they had taken from guards. Dear God ... that is what they wanted from me! If Martha and her kids hadn't been there, they would have made me go with them to be able to interpret what was being said on the radios. It would have destroyed my life and my children's lives, and undoubtedly, Gary also would have killed me once he got what he needed. Through faith my mother had always instilled in me, I always had guardian angels around me, protecting me from harm ... and this night, they were working overtime.

After the fact, and with much thought, I believed in my heart that Donnie Joe thought the boys and his father was going straight to Mexico where Dorothy would join them and live as a family ... *happy ever after.* I believe in his heart, Donnie Joe thought once they got to the Mexico border, Gary would have turned me loose, if they had taken me that Saturday night, as I'm sure Gary told him he would, as surely as I know in my heart, he and Dorothy sent the boys to take me that night to interpret the codes for the police radio after they had escaped. We all know that Gary was a cold-blooded killer with no remorse and would have killed me as well once he didn't need me anymore, despite what Donnie Joe would have said or done, becoming obvious from statements made after Ricky and Raymond's arrest, they had absolutely no control over what Gary did or didn't do. He was insane and without a doubt, on a rampage once he escaped from the prison.

When this realization finally sunk in after the escape and we learned they had taken radios with them, Martha and I figured out why the boys had come by my apartment that Saturday night, I became physically sick. All I wanted to do was hug my kids and thank God for his protection and Martha for being there that night.

Once again, the Angels of Mercy protected my family and me ....

Chapter 14
Day of Escape
July 28, 1978

My kids and I decided to attend church with my sister, Martha, on that Sunday, which was unusual for us since we attended St. Anthony's. My two younger kids decided to ride with their Aunt Martha to her house in Maricopa from church where we'd have lunch then head to the Francisco Grande for a car show that all the kids were looking forward to. As I headed toward Maricopa with my oldest son, riding with me, we had just past Thornton Road on the Maricopa Highway heading west when I saw a police officer was going to pull me over. I assumed I was speeding, as did my sister, and she kept driving so she wouldn't also get a speeding ticket and told me later she was chuckling, as she continued to drive.

As the officer got out of his patrol vehicle, I noticed in my rear-view mirror that he was going to do a felony stop, which I was familiar with from working at the local police department as a dispatcher and matron. During my training period, the officers would have dispatchers ride along as training so they could know what the officers were experiencing out in the public and know when to call for back-up. I quickly recognized what was considered a felony stop. I was confused to say the least, also personally knowing the office standing behind my vehicle, however before I had a chance to attempt to figure this out, another patrol car sped in front of me, stopping at an angle, blocking my car, and throwing dust everywhere, then two more police vehicles coming up at a high rate of speed, also stopping abruptly, again, throwing dust everywhere. The officer behind me got out of his vehicle with his gun drawn. I notice through the rear-view mirror that the police officer behind me used his knee to see if he could open the trunk, also with his gun drawn. All I could think of was, "What the hell has one of my brothers' done now!?"

My son had been six feet since he was 12 years old and looked older for his age. I told him, "I don't have any clue what is going on here, but please do whatever they say to do, follow their instructions and be polite, do not say anything unless asked a question" all the while trying to sound calm for his sake. By now, there were numerous other officers on the scene, and it was getting scary, however trying to stay brave for my son who was obviously as terrified as I was.

I turned from the rear-view mirror to look toward the passenger side, and I saw an officer had walked up quickly and put a gun to my son's head, telling him "Put your hands on the dash. What is your name?" He told the officer his name and he was terrified as was I. At this point, my only concern was that this officer had a gun to my son's head.

The officer on the driver's side instructed me to put my hands on the steering wheel, turn off the vehicle with my left hand and open the door with my right arm. He also asked if I had any weapons. I told him no, reminded him that he knew me, then did as he instructed. By now, I was crying and begging them to please remove the gun pointed at my son's head but to no avail. Before exiting the vehicle, I told my son again to sit very still and do exactly what they asked, assuring him he would be all right. As bad as this all was, the officer with the gun to my son's head kept shifting from leg to leg in a nervous manner, much like a Barney Fife type. You could tell he wanted to shoot someone, anyone, who was affiliated with the escape or the Tisons, and of course at that point I didn't even know about the escape. This officer obvious wanted to shoot someone, judging from his actions, that he wanted to be a hero in the public's eye and would go to great lengths to do so. I again cautioned my son to do whatever they said to do and not to make any sudden moves.

As soon as I exited the vehicle, I was practically dragged to the rear of my vehicle by several officers and thrown up against the trunk and handcuffed. I'm crying profusely, asking what I had done and please get the gun from my son's head. I was told "Shut the fuck up, you Tison bitch." What was so terrifying to me was that I had always tried to shield my children from any type of Tison behavioral repercussions or actions, yet here was my son with a gun to his head. I had never told my children what a horrific lifestyle I had growing up, about the police always being at our house, prison terms for my father and brothers, but encouraged them always to stay clear of my brothers and their families as they simply weren't good people, I had told them they had a different lifestyle than we had and could be a bad influence on them. Until Gary escaped from prison, and it was all over the news and my brothers and father's history were all out in the open for everyone to hear and see due to the news media, including my sons, they had no clue just how bad it had been growing up with these men. DeAnna was too young to understand, however, I caught my boy's numerous times watching the news, and of course, they recapped the entire family history. I would attempt to find other ways for them to be entertained rather than listening to this horrible thing on the news ... and they were horrible, however I had no control over my father or brothers' actions over the years or the news media recapping it repeatedly.

After what seemed forever and a hundred questions about where I had been earlier in the day and who was the young man in the front seat, I was taken out of handcuffs but told to stand still, which of course I did. The one officer told me I was going to drive my car to the local police department, but they would be in front and back of me and if I tried to run away, they would shoot me. I was simply happy the one officer had removed the gun from my son's head and would have agreed to anything. After what seemed like hours, they finally asked him if he had any I.D. He slowly took his wallet out; his young hands were shaking so badly that he had a hard time getting his school I.D. out of his wallet. We still had no clue as to why we were being detained and treated in this manner, but it became apparent, nobody was going to answer any of my questions.

My sister had gone onto Maricopa, and she had absolutely no idea what was going on, and I had no way of contacting her as they wouldn't allow me to call her once we arrived at the police department.

The trip to the CGPD seemed to take forever, as I was afraid if I drove too fast, they would think I was trying to get away and knew without a doubt, at least one of them, possibly all of them, desperately wanted to shoot us. There were two police cars in front of me, and I believe four behind me, all with their lights on. Some friends recognized my car on this little trip to the police department and looked stunned, not knowing what was happening. People were pulling over to the side of the road, stopping due to all the police cars and lights. It was so humiliating, yet I was still terrified and concerned mostly about my son who was, without a doubt, being traumatized.

When arriving at the local police department I was again handcuffed when I got out of my vehicle, while another officer escorted my son into another room. I sat in a chair for what seemed like hours until several officers including prison officers came in and told me that my brother, Gary, had escaped from prison earlier, along with Randy Greenwalt with the help of his three sons, and in a similar make and model vehicle that I was driving. One of the higher-ranking officers from the prison was extremely aggressive and was yelling in my face. He insisted I knew of the escape, had assisted, and knew where Gary, his sons and Randy Greenwalt were and said, "That boy in the other room is probably one of Gary's sons." I kept trying to assure him he was not, that he was my son and we'd just come from church and one of the officers had seen his school I.D. I didn't have any clue as to what they were talking about and knew nothing of the escape until they told me. I had been at church with my children, sister, and her children. However, I knew during this entire ordeal from the time I was stopped, from experiencing, growing up with the Tisons, that one of my brothers had done something again, this time, apparently bad.

Growing up in my household as a child, it wasn't unusual for the police to come to our house for one reason or another. It was never good. Once when I was about 8 years old, two officers were at the door and I yelled to my mother "The cops are here looking for my brothers," before they even asked, didn't even know which one, but it was always one of them, if not all of them. My father was a career criminal, never keeping a job long and we were always moving from one place to another because he got mad at his boss for some reason or another or involved in some sort of criminal activity. I'd hear him telling our mother what an ass the boss was, and how he didn't have to take that shit. And we would move again. He would make fast money whenever the opportunity was there for him, and he taught his sons to do the same.

Gary had been in and out of prison most of my life since I was incredibly young, and Larry was young, only eighteen months older than I and was being strongly influenced by my father and brothers, as I later learned. I had always believed that mother had a stronger influence on Larry than our father, but later, I learned I was wrong.

***

Back to the eventful day of the Escape: Two additional Arizona State Prison officials came into the room they were holding me in. One of the prison officials walked right up to me and punched me in the face with a closed fist, and I could feel blood running and knew he had loosened a couple teeth. I begged him to please stop, but he responded with yet another punch, this one even harder. With my hands being cuffed behind me, there wasn't anything I could do except sit there and take it, trying to avoid taking a direct hit.

My jaw had been wired together for months after Raymond beat the crap out of me in Key West years prior, I was afraid this prison official hit me exactly right, it would break it again, so I turned trying to dodge the direct hit. He kept insisting I knew where Gary was, and he was going to beat it out of me. I once again tried to tell him I didn't know anything about the escape, Gary, or anything else and had been with my children in church. About the time he was to deliver the third punch to my face, Sgt. Stanford, chief of detectives by then, walked in and said to the prison officer, more calmly that I wanted him to "If you hit her again, I'll shoot you myself." He was always a soft-spoken man but had a reputation for being tough, and apparently the prison officer knew his reputation. The guy backed off but told him I knew where they were. He said, "I know her, she is a friend, and I can tell you, she doesn't know anything, she isn't like them. She doesn't even hardly know Gary even though he is her brother." The prison official didn't like this and said it was his investigation and he would handle it anyway he saw fit. Sgt. Stanford made it abundantly clear he wouldn't, it was his police department and reiterated that if he hit me again, he would shoot him. I could tell from the look in his eyes, that he might possibly do it. At this point, I honestly was wishing he would, I would have felt a lot safer if he had just shot this prison official who was beating me in my face, while handcuffed to a chair.

Sgt. Stanford took the handcuffs off me and told me to go into the bathroom and wash up and meet him in his office, which I immediately did. Although I did ask him to make sure this prison official didn't follow me into the restroom and to find my son. He assured me the only place this son of a bitch was going was out the door or into a jail cell, but to be safe, Sgt. Stanford had an officer stand by the door to make sure nobody went into the Ladies Room while I was in there. He was shocked to learn my son had even there and immediately found him and took him into his office.

Sgt. Stanford asked me if I wanted something to drink when I came back into his office, I noticed they had already gotten my son a soda from the machine and was trying to calm him down, as we were both terrorized. He took me into his private office and explained the details of the escape and kept apologizing for the way the local police and prison officials had acted and for the abuse I had taken. He noticed that two of my teeth to the front right side were loose and told me to go to a dentist the following day and bring him the bill, that the state would be paying for it. He explained to me that he knew I wasn't a part of this but had to ask certain questions such as; did I have any knowledge of this escape prior to it happening, etc. I assured him I didn't, but that Joe had boasted once at my sister's house that he was going to get Gary out. In my mother's simple thinking and Christian innocence, I'm sure she thought he was going to use a lawyer, not his sons and guns as it went down.

This was only the beginning of what became a living nightmare for me, my children and other innocent family members which lasted for years and sometimes still surfaces after forty plus years. The eleven days of the manhunt for Gary was a nightmare one could only imagine. We were more afraid of Gary than the public, but nobody realized that; they assumed because he was our brother, we would help him. Nothing could have been further from the truth.

It was like watching a horror movie and you couldn't turn it off …. unfortunately, we were living it.

When I was finally able to call my sister, I asked her to please bring my other two kids home. She, of course, had already learned of the escape but had no idea of what we had live through that day. I desperately needed my kids to be with me, I knew I had to keep them safe. I knew Gary was a cold-blooded killer and was more desperate now than ever before. I had already figured out why Donnie Joe and Ricky had come to my apartment the day before, to take me to interpret the codes on the radio. I had told in detail, Sgt. Stanford about them coming to my home the previous night and he agreed whole heartedly, that they had planned to take me to interrupt the codes while on the run. As desperate as they were, I figured they were hopefully smart enough not to come back to Casa Grande or anywhere near us. I just needed to be with my kids and keep them as safe as I possibly could. I walked out of my apartment later that day to have a cigarette and saw an unmarked police car sitting at the entrance to my apartment complex. I assumed they would stay there all night; little did I know at the time, he and other officers were with me the entire eleven days of the manhunt. They were covering every possible place Gary and his gang might show up, and I was so grateful they were there as Donnie Joe and Ricky both knew where I lived since, they had been there the day prior. I put my kids in the bed with me and noticed how restless my oldest son was after what he had been through that horrific day. I laid my hand on his back while he slept, as he was whimpering throughout the night, I kept assuring him that I would keep them all safe. We finally all drifted off to sleep, but I woke early to listen to the news hoping they had already been captured.

Unfortunately, not and it was all that was on the news. As the kids got up, I turned off the TV and made breakfast, trying to comfort them and talk about anything except the prior day.

Chapter 15
Day 2 After Escape

The days following the escape were a nightmare for everyone, especially the family. We were more afraid of Gary than anyone however some assumed because he was our brother, we would help him. Nothing could have been further from the truth. Us girls were terrified of him growing up and even more so now, as we knew he was desperate with every law enforcement officer in this part of the United States looking for him, his sons and Randy.

My sisters and I that we were followed wherever we went after the escape, and I honestly found great comfort in that. I knew with an officer nearby, if Gary tried to make contact, they would get him before he got to us. My older sister, Martha, and I went to the airport to pick up our other sister coming from Oklahoma and realized this unmarked car which had been parked outside my apartment since right after the escape, was following close behind me all the way to the airport.

As sad as it sounds, after years of driving an ambulance, I had become accustomed to driving way too fast. As tough as the job was, it was nice to have lights and sirens to speed to the next call, however when in my private vehicle, I had to use caution and remind myself that I wasn't in an ambulance and didn't have red lights and a siren. After Gary's escape, I soon realized that I wasn't going to be stopped because the officers who followed assumed or hoped we were going to meet Gary and his gang, which couldn't have been further from the truth. I took full advantage of this opportunity of driving fast, as we were late getting to the airport. Once we picked up our sister, we went to a local coffee shop to get something to eat and attempted to fill her in on our fears and what had taken place thus far. She was very sympathetic to what had happened to me and my son the day of the escape and just kept crying, as I told her about this horrific experience. The unmarked police vehicle sat in the parking lot the entire time, upon leaving I took him a cup of coffee and a breakfast sandwich, telling him "I know you have a job to do, but you must be hungry. I'll drive slowly so you can eat while you follow us. Have a blessed day." He looked somewhat shocked but thanked me and took both.

My sister from Oklahoma chose to stay with our mother, which was great as mother was beside herself, as one could expect. It was also a blessing for me as well since I could be with my kids all the time and not have to worry about mother. This didn't last for long though, as she chose to be with Dorothy for whatever reason. They had grown up together and were friends as young girls, but for the life of me, I couldn't understand why she would leave our mother and go be with Dorothy. I had already determined in my own mind that Dorothy was up to her neck in this whole escape, and truth be known she planned the entire thing. As it turned out, I was right, she had done just that and sent her own sons into a prison with weapons to break out Gary and his co-hart Randy, who was a known killer. My God! What kind of a mother would do this!?

Mother even quit going to church during this time as

even church people thought she might have some *good in-formation* they could spread to others, something perhaps that hadn't been on the news. My mother, like the rest of us, knew nothing about this escape, where they were or what they were planning. Only fear that they would show up at one of our homes for help.

Even though they had been close growing up, I tried to tell my sister that Dorothy was responsible for this, en-abling her sons to help Gary escape. I was lost in my thoughts as "what the hell type mother would put her child-ren in that position. And where the hell was she the day of the escape, we didn't see her over at the state prison with a shotgun in her hand" .... she sent her sons to do her dirty work. Despite our advice to stay clear of Dorothy, my sister insisted on being with her.

I was living in Hacienda de Kadota apartments with my children, working and trying to get my life together again after dear brother, Joe got me fired from both the police department and my ambulance job. I ultimately lost my home and had to move into the apartment. So here I was again, starting over thanks to my brother, Joe.

When we returned from the airport, Martha went home to Maricopa and after taking my other sister to my moth-er's, I decided I needed to be with my children. They had been staying with my dear friend, Sharon, who I'd asked to keep her TV and radio off due to the news considering this escape and manhunt was constantly on the news. She helped me considerably during this time with my children and tried to help me keep my sanity; I always will be grateful to her for her friendship in such a time of need.

When I arrived back at the apartment, my daughter asked me if she could go play on the swings. A few moments later, I was told by a hysterical neighbor that someone was hurting my daughter, the lady kept screaming and pointing towards the swing area. I ran to the playground to find the assistant manager and his sons had pulled DeAnna off the swing by her feet and dragged her across the hot rocks, telling her she wasn't allowed to play there because her uncle was a murderer. None of us at the time even know about the murders of the Lyons family in Quartzsite or the young recently married couple in Colorado; he obviously was referring to the prison guard Gary had killed years prior. Whatever his thoughts or reasoning was, he was hurting my daughter, and I just about came unglued.

This assistant manager of the apartment complex was a strange man and always walking around the complex twirling his keys around his fingers to impress tenants and remind them he had a master key to every apartment. His overweight and lazy sons, in their mid-teens, appeared to be as ignorant and arrogant as he was and always walking right behind him. He had most likely never had a job before where he had any authority, and he let it go to his head. Most, including myself, just ignored him until today.

Dear Lord, this was a nightmare and out of control, but my only thought was getting medical treatment for my little girl. Sharon again took my boys to her apartment and assured me she would watch them closely. I took DeAnna to the emergency room, and as she was being treated, I just stood there holding her little hand and wondering why this was happening and why would a grown man want to hurt an innocent little girl. She was so scared; she was badly scratched up, and bleeding in several areas on her legs and hips. The doctors literally had to pull pieces of rocks from her skin.

Having been in and out of the hospital so much with my ambulance work, I knew many of the staff. I always laughed and joked with them, but this time, only stood there in total shock. One nurse remembered that I was good friends with Sgt. Stanford and called him to tell him what had happened. I learned later that he was in the Phoenix area but headed back with red lights and siren in his unmarked vehicle, as soon as he received the nurse's call, he immediately came to the hospital. He assured me he would make a formal complaint on my behalf of the assistant manager and his son, as he considered it Assault on a Child, a felony. He just asked that I give him time to contact the county attorney for charges and promised me he would arrest them both himself.

After hours of treatment, I took my daughter home and had Sharon bring the boys back home. She too lived in the apartment complex upstairs from where we lived. After Sharon left, I explained to the kids that people could be mean and cruel, and that Sgt. Stanford was filing criminal charges on those who had hurt DeAnna and hopefully they wouldn't bother us again. But I also cautioned them intensely about staying close to the apartment, not being anywhere except inside or where I could hear and see them right outside the door. At that point, they too were afraid and agreed to stay close by me.

My oldest son had a morning paper route, I sat outside with him early in the morning wrapping newspapers. I assumed, being the fat and lazy folks that they were, the Assistant manager, and his sons were, they wouldn't be up this early and my son would be safe from them. Boy, was I wrong! Apparently, they knew he had a paper route and was waiting for him in the front complex. The three of them, manager and his two sons, pulled him off his bike and dragged him to the pool where they held his head under water, attempting to drown him while continually yelling "Your uncle is a murderer, so we're going to kill you." What saved him was an old man heard the commotion and ran out to the pool area to help him. He got hurt in the struggle but was able to get my son to safety. He brought him home with his bike and I called the police. Sgt. Stanford heard the call and immediately headed to my apartment. He came screaming around the corner with tires squealing when he saw me heading to the Assistance Manager's apartment with gun in hand. I was hysterical and determined to avenge my son and what they had done to my daughter and prevent them from hurting my kids again. I had an old Saturday Night Special I had kept in a shoe box way in the back of the closet with the bullets stored elsewhere. My previous husband, Raymond had given it to me years prior and I forgot I had it until that day. I wasn't sure exactly what I was going to do, shoot them or just scare them into leaving my children alone, but I knew this had to end, and I was desperate to act. The ol' Mama Bear thing and all. What I didn't give thought to at the time, was that I looked as bad as my brothers, storming down to their apartment with a gun in my hand. I was hysterical to say the least and just wanted this to stop before they seriously hurt one of my kids.

Sgt. Stanford jumped out of his car and instructed me to hand him the gun I had swinging from my hand as I was

quickly walked towards their apartment. He slowly removed the gun from my hand and assured me that he
would deal with them. He promised, as my friend, that if he
couldn't get justice for what they had done to my daughter
and son, he would shoot them himself. I honestly believe
that at this moment because he was as upset as I'd ever
seen him, almost in tears himself. He assured me my children and I had done nothing wrong, but the world was full of
ignorant people and felt we were guilty by relationship. I
handed him the gun and went back to my apartment while
he angrily spoke with them. He said he assured them if they
in anyway attempted to contact me or one of my children
again, he would arrest them himself. He told them he
already contacted the county attorney office and charges
were coming for Child Endangerment, as to what they had
done to DeAnna. He told them that Attempted Murder was
now going to be charged as well for holding my son's head
under water. What he didn't tell me at the time was that this
in no way affected them; they were arrogant and determined to get what they called "justice" through innocent
children who had never even met Gary.

He asked me if I had another place I could stay, strongly
indicating both my kids and I were in danger, but I told him
I didn't. My mother lived in a small one-bedroom apartment, and there simply wasn't room. Out of desperation
and safety for my kids, I called some friends and stayed
with them for the next couple of days. When you live
through an ordeal such as this, you surely find out who your
true friends are.

I returned a couple days later to retrieve some more
clothing for the kids and me, and when I got to the door, I

realized it had been kicked in. Assuming the assistant manager had done this was confusing since he had a master key. Was totally unnecessary to kick in the door? I suppose he was attempting to make a point, even though he had a master key to all apartments. When I walked inside, I couldn't believe what I saw. The place was trashed, broken dishes, TV and on the wall in spray paint was written "Tison Bitch Move Out." As frightened as I was, I managed to put some more clothing in a bag and locate a padlock, not that there was a lot left to protect, but I felt it necessary to protect what little I did have left. With the help of a neighbor guy and his drill, we got it installed, and he told me the assistant manager and his sons had done this, he watched them do it. I asked him why he hadn't called the police, and he just shrugged and said he didn't want to get involved. Wow ... Seriously!

At this point, I knew I couldn't take my children back to this apartment because apparently, we were all in great danger, not from Gary and his gang, but this assistant manager and his sons.

I had been dating this man from the Phoenix area and finally called and told him what had happened and was there any way he could help me, as I knew I couldn't continue to stay with my friends, and money was limited with me. They had said it was fine and they were gracious, but we were living a nightmare and I didn't want to impose any more than I already had. All the news was about the escape and manhunt, and there was an unmarked car sitting outside their home. I always had been independent but was desperate at this point to do or go anywhere my kids and I would be safe. My friend was there within an hour and said he had already rented two adjoining rooms via phone at the Francisco Grande Resort and had instructed them to remove the radio and TV from one of the rooms. His thoughts were that I could control what the kids watched in my room, without them seeing the news, however I could stay informed. He said I could stay there with my kids for as long as I needed to; we could swim with the kids, eat in the restaurant, do fun things with them, and keep them away from all this, and he knew I'd be safe there and he would not have to worry about me. He suggested I not let anyone know where I was or tell anyone I was while staying there. This all came as a welcome surprise to me, as I had no idea, he had that kind of money. He said he put it on a major credit card, and it would be taken care of. I didn't question it; I was just relieved I could take my children to a safer place and no longer must impose on my dear friends who had graciously opened their home to us.

I tried to make it a fun little "secret" with the kids that nobody could know we were related to Gary and what had happened in our apartment or to either of them. It was little "our secret," and they promised to keep it. Although I rarely let them out of my sight and if someone were talking to them at the pool or anywhere else, I would always go up to them and ask them not to. I got a lot of weird looks from people, one lady saying, "I was only trying to be nice." My response was simply "Be nice to someone else." but I had to be extremely cautious. This had turned into one of the biggest manhunts in the western parts of the United States, and everyone knew about it, watched daily news and of course, everyone had their own take on it all. My goal was simply to keep my mother and my kids safe.

Once again, you truly find out who your true friends are when faced with a situation such as we were living through. One of my dear friends and her family offered to take my kids on field trips to the zoo, others horseback riding and different places out of town just to keep them occupied while I went to check on mother. Nobody realized where I was but would meet them either in town or take the kids to their homes when offering to do activities with them and immediately go to mom's. Of course, the officer who had been following me, also followed me and knew I was there. Again, it gave me a sense of safety.

I asked mother if she would please come to the Francisco Grande and stay with us, but she refused, saying she wasn't going to leave her apartment. I asked in the sweetest voice I could muster if Gary had contacted her. She assured me he hadn't. I again, lovingly told her that if he did, she was going to have to report it or at the very least, tell me. She became incredibly angry at me and told me if they knew where he was, they would kill him. I asked her if she knew Gary had already killed several innocent people, and she cried, saying she was praying for them and their families and was sick about it, not believing Gary could do such a thing. I reminded her that he shot a defenseless prison guard years ago for no reason; he could have just left him in the desert, but he killed him instead. When being led out of the courtroom years prior, Dorothy, pretending to hug Gary, slipped him a gun which he used to overpower the guard who had transported him, killed him in the desert and left him to die. However, I tried to make her understand that if he weren't caught, more innocent people could die. She said, "I know what Gary has done, but you must understand, he is my son." I held her close while she cried but assured her, she had to let me know if he contacted her before anyone else died at his hands. She promised me she would tell me, but I wasn't entirely sure she would.

The sheriff found out where I was staying and called me asking for a meeting. I assumed the officers that had me under surveillance had reported I had moved myself and kids into the Francisco Grande. When he finally got through to my room, he chuckled and said, "I had one hell of a time getting through to you, as they refused to put my call through until I told them I was Pinal County Sheriff Frank Reyes." I explained to him I had asked them not to put calls through due to so many news reporters wanting to ask questions. He said he understood. He said my mother had to be questioned and he was going to do it himself and asked if I wanted to be present, I assured him I did. I had told him about our conversation the day prior as to whether Gary had contacted her or not. He said she still needed to be questioned by law enforcement, as all other family members had, and he felt he could be compassionate to her while doing so. We agreed to meet at her apartment the following day.

I arrived first and was just getting out of my car when a news reporter van had pulled up and a guy jumped out informing me, I was Gary's sister, like I didn't already know that and wanted to interview me. I asked them to leave but to no avail. I decided to get back into my car and wait for Frank Reyes. However, this news reporter was aggressive and kept pounding on my driver's side window, yelling at me to open the door or window so we could talk, all the while his cameraman was filming. He and his crew got in front of my car and keep taping me with his camera. I started the car and slowly ran into him, just tapping him, trying to get him to leave me alone. He was screaming at me at this point and threatened to have me arrested for assault by hitting him with the front of my car. I knew I hadn't hurt him, only wanted to scare him away. When the sheriff arrived a few minutes later, he ran up to him saying he wanted to file a complaint on me and wanted me arrested. The sheriff informed this reporter in no uncertain terms, that if they didn't leave immediately that he would have his deputies come and arrest them. I realized my poor mother was watching this whole ordeal from her front door. As the news reporter pointed the camera at her, I immediately walked back away from the sheriff up to where the news reporter was standing and filming and knocked it out of his hand; when it hit the ground, it broke into numerous pieces. He promised to sue me. I quietly reminded him of who I was, Gary Tison's sister, having the same blood running through my veins as he had, and discouraged any lawsuit of any kind. I told him to leave and erase what he had just filmed of my mother standing in the doorway with the sheriff walking in her direction. The sheriff apparently heard what I had said to him, put his arm around my shoulder and chuckled saying, "I think you got his attention; I don't think he'll use the footage he got," as he chuckled. I only used this Tison thing as leverage when I had no alternative, as I explained to the sheriff, and this seemed to be one of those appropriate times. He said he understood and was still chuckling. I never did see it on the news, so apparently, he took me seriously and as a threat from a Tison. I'm not a criminal, never have been, and never done anything with a criminal intent. However, it was as though I stepped out of myself for a few moments and used my relationship to Gary as an advantage. I would go to any lengths to protect mother or my children.

As we walked inside, the sheriff shook my mom's hand and told her it was a privilege to meet her. He was gracious and kind, and you can't imagine how much that meant to me as I knew he was going to ask her a series of questions. She told us she had made a coconut cream pie and made iced tea and informed him it was RC's favorite pie. I'm sure like myself, he could have cared less as we both knew RC's history of criminal activity and could care less that this was his favorites. She asked him if he wanted some tea and pie, he said he did, so we sat at her kitchen table. He said, "You do know who I am and why I am here."

"Yes, Lynda told me," she responded. While pouring us a glass of tea, she told him, "I'm going to tell you what I told Lynda yesterday. Gary hasn't called me, and I don't know where he is."

His next question caused a distressed look on her face when he asked her if she would call either him or myself if he did in any way attempt to contact her.

She abruptly said, "No because you will kill him."

As he ate his pie and drank iced tea, he assured her it was his job to find Gary, his boys and would do everything in his power to bring them in without hurting them.

She asked him if he was serious, and he took her hand and assured her he was.

I knew he was being dishonest with her, but desperate times call for desperate measures, and he desperately needed to apprehend Gary and his gang. She promised to tell me if he called or made any kind of contact with her, which was a tremendous relief to us both, although I didn't believe Gary would contact her because his goal was to kill our brother Joe for betraying him and go to Mexico. He surely wasn't going to risk seeing his mother when every law enforcement officer in the western part of the United States was looking for him.

I was extremely pleased by the way the sheriff handled this interview with my mother. Although she was my mother, who I loved completely, she was also the mother of the notorious Gary Tison. This could have been handled so badly if not for my friendship with this sheriff and his compassion for an old lady who unfortunately was Gary's mother, who had no say in how he was influenced by RC growing up.

The sheriff said his goodbyes to mother, and I walked him outside. I hugged and thanked him for handling this so gently. He said, "Of course, which is why I handled it myself." Became obvious to me that he desperately needed to find Gary and his gang but also had a heart of compassion because this could have been a bad situation for my mother. He also chuckled again about the reporter and said, "I doubt he'll be back."

About a year later after this interview by the sheriff at my mother's apartment, I was hosting a fashion show to raise money for some local organization and had seated my mother at the front table, right next to the sheriff. When I took the podium, I almost choked realizing what I had done, but it was too late to make any changes. I couldn't exactly go down and move my mother to another table. I never liked public speaking anyway, even though I have spent many years raising funds for abused children and different organizations, but this time was even worse for me, as I realized others were quietly making comments about the head table. .... Gary Tison's mother seated next to the sheriff, as the news was still actively reporting on the Tison and the escape even a year later. He winked at me as to say, *"don't worry about these small-minded idiots"* and nodded his head as if he were saying *"proceed"*. I pulled myself together and introduced the officials present and then my precious mother. After the show had ended, the sheriff came up to me, taking hold of my hands and said, "Thank you for seating me next to your mother; what an honor it was for me." Wow, you talk about respect – I had nothing but respect for this sheriff and still do because he was so gracious when it came to my mother. I just learned recently that he had passed, and I felt I had lost a good friend, and it made my heart sad. I quietly said, "Adios my friend," while reading his Obituary and tears running down my cheeks. I saw him on numerous occasions over the years, even having a fundraiser at my ranch for himself and one of the County Attorney's years later during election season. As I made my rounds to different tables to thank everyone for attending and to remind everyone to donate generously, he pulled out a beer from an ice chest and said, "Take a break," took my hand and said, "We've come a long way since your mother's kitchen table years ago." He often would stop by my ranch and have a beer with me, or we would have lunch somewhere in the county. He and I would chuckle about the fact that some others thought it was strange we were such good friends, and always introduced me as his good friend, Lynda as folks would approach out table in restaurants.

When my late husband, Frank had his first bout with throat cancer many years ago, some friends and I had traveled to Jamaica. While there I learned a lot about the medicinal purpose in so many of their plants. I had several seeds sent home to Arizona, but unlike Jamaica, Arizona it was hot and dry, and they needed moisture to thrive. I purchased three swamp coolers after planting the seeds in pots on my patio and ran the three swamp coolers onto them in a diagonal angle, hoping they would think they were growing in Jamaica in that nice moist air. I was successful, and as the plants grew, I would hang them to dry, then afterwards put them in capsules or daily drinks for Frank's recovery from cancer. Apparently, I was successful as it was more than twenty years before the cancer returned.

One day the sheriff stopped by on his way home, grabbed a beer for us both out of the beer-fridge in the garage and walked out to the pasture while I was putting away a horse, then we both headed towards the patio. As he walked around the house toward the patio, he saw all those plants growing. He immediately said "Wow," thinking at first glance that they were marijuana plants. He turned to look at me with a grin and said, "You do know I'm still the Sheriff right." I laughed and assured him there wasn't a damn thing growing that one could smoke and explained my trip to Jamaica and what I had learned about the health benefits of many of their plants and that I was helping my Frank on his journey to rid himself of cancer. I also told him of growing up so poor and that my mother had always used natural healing plants due to not being able to afford doctors and such. He listened intently and then said, "If I ever get sick, I'm coming here." Shortly after, my Frank, my husband showed up, and we enjoyed a couple more beers and talked about my plants. My Frank was a typical cowboy and was somewhat embarrassed that I was using plant leaves to heal him, however, he also knew they were effective, and was grateful for my efforts and told the sheriff as much.

***

Going back a few years, before marrying Frank, my friend Tim and I had been dating, and he helped me buy a nice older home on Kadota Avenue. He bought it for me and reiterated that my kids and I would be safer, and it was obvious I couldn't go back to my apartment. He hired movers to go retrieve the rest of my belongings – what little was left – to the new house. We had been at the Francisco Grande for more than two weeks. The new house Tim bought for us was in a good neighborhood and close to La Grande Pool, which my kids loved, and we thought, good neighbors. The house had a large, fenced back yard so we trimmed trees and shrubs, put up swings and a bench swing on the little patio and it felt safe and was becoming home. The house needed lots of repairs, but I was surely up to the task of drowning myself in hard work and staying out of public places. He opened an account in my name at Foxworth Store and a couple other places so I could purchase what I needed for repairs, paint, carpet, etc. He also told me I shouldn't worry about going back to work for a while, as most likely nobody was going to hire me anyway and he said he would take care of me and the kids for a as long as it took. Imagine my surprise as once again, I had no idea he had that sort of money, but apparently, he did and was willing to help me. I mentioned earlier that I believe that angels come in many forms, and he was one of them.

While the kids and I were cleaning, and painting two young kids came to the door and asked if I'd sign a petition. When looking at it, I was shocked to see it was a petition being signed by everyone in the neighborhood to prevent "A Tison" from moving there, assuming I was renting and didn't know Tim had already purchased the home for me. I also assumed their parents hadn't told them which house *NOT* to go to. I told them I'd keep it, look over it, and return it to tomorrow, learning they lived right behind me on the next street. The kids didn't have a problem with that since they were in their swimsuits. I assumed they were headed to La Grande Pool and were happy to be finished for the day. I immediately called Tim, and he was so angry that someone in this neighborhood would take it upon themselves to do this. He came down from the metro area right away, picked up the petition, and took it to a lawyer, and the lawyer himself delivered it back to its originator and made it abundantly clear if anything like this happened again, he would file a lawsuit against them and anyone who signed it. I've watched this family who circulated this petition over the years, and it reminds me of how horrible Karma can be, as they had nothing but problems, both financially and with their kids, etc. That petition came back to bite them throughout the years.

Karma is a bitch.

Knowing I had little to no options for moving forward, I kept my head high, trying to do the right thing and raising my children. Things had gotten better, as I found a good job working for a cotton breeding company and started doing some investments on distressed properties thanks to Tim .... life seem to be moving along well, despite those who periodically threw the Tison thing in my face. I had even been able to purchase a 26' motorhome so I could take the kids on trips and spend some time in San Diego, which was without any doubt, our favorite place. Staying in the RV allowed me to cook meals and cut cost considerably and once again, felt I had accomplished yet another of my goals and feeling good about myself.

One afternoon shortly after I came home from work, Joe showed up after being released from yet another federal prison saying he needed a place to stay. Holy shit, I immediately thought, there was no way he was going to live with me and my kids! He had another idea altogether. He pleaded with me to borrow my RV and assured me he was only going to live in it for a couple weeks in San Diego, as he had a good job offer. He promised that once he started working, he would return my RV and even be able to pay me for the use of it. In retrospect, how can one human be so stupid as to fall for this Tison bullshit again, but I did!

Two weeks after Joe borrow it, I received a call from California Highway Patrol saying they had impounded my RV. The towing, impound fees, etc. were exuberant. I sat on the patio thinking how stupid I was to think Joe was trying to do what was right by getting a job and just needing my RV for a place to sleep and shower. I flew over, took a cab, and went to California Highway Patrol Division, paid all the fines, and retrieved my RV.

As I walked through it while still in CHP impound lot, I got chills thinking about what had most likely gone on in the rig while Joe had it. It made me sick to my stomach, which was a familiar situation when dealing with some members of my family. Most all the paneling had been removed to hide illegals, a hole had been cut out under the bed for smuggling drugs, and it was in extremely bad shape. I stopped at a supermarket, bought cleaning supplies and gloves, as it also smelled bad, and I wasn't sure if there might not be something in it that I could catch. I drove to the beach, opened it up and started cleaning. As I drove the RV back to Casa Grande, I was thoroughly disgusted with myself more than anyone for trusting yet another of the Tisons and vowed it would never happen again.

The nightmare of my brother's criminal activities, especially Gary's escape continued for years to come, even sometimes after all these years, it still surfaces and I'm usually blindsided when it does, even as recently as front-page news in the Tri-Valley Dispatch with pictures as recently as December 2020. My brothers and father were career criminals, and my family and I had to reap the devastating results of it all. As bad as it was from the escape, it didn't end there, I had two other brothers and they continued in their life of crime, as always, include front page news articles and TV news, bringing even more shame and disgrace to innocent victims of our remaining family members.

Chapter 16
Day 3 After Escape

In early 1978, Joe drove up to my younger sister's house in Tulsa, Okla., in a purple-colored Lincoln Continental. He told her there were guns in the trunk, and he was going to have to leave it there for a couple days before he could drive it to Arizona. He told her that he promised Gary that he would provide a car and guns as Dorothy and their sons were going to break Gary out of prison later in the year. He assured her they were all too stupid to pull something like this off, but he promised Gary, due to threats made against his wife and kids if he didn't and was only keeping his promise. Even being the bad guy Joe was, he along with the rest of our family had always feared Gary and for good reason. Gary was probably the only person Joe was afraid of. Gary was a sociopath with no conscience and with one blue eye and one hazel; he was just frightening to look at.

Joe told my sister he was going to put it into a storage facility in the Phoenix area and they could have it, after all, it hadn't cost him anything so he said, but still didn't think they could pull it off. But he said it wasn't his problem. Of course, his statement that it hadn't cost anything indicated the damn car was probably stolen and now it was sitting in her front yard ... with guns in the trunk so he had said. The whole scenario frightening as hell, she called me crying, not knowing what to do. Of course, nobody ever said "No" to Joe, as we fearfully learned growing up, it's just the way it always was.

My sister was devastated, as she hadn't seen Joe in years, and was surprised he even knew where they lived considering they had just moved into a newly constructed home on the outskirts of Tulsa, pretty much in the country, isolated and hard to find. Keeping in mind, we didn't have cell phones, GPS and all the other gadgets we used today to locate people and places at that time. The fact that he just left the vehicle, threatened her if she bothered it, looked inside, etc., and then took off was frightening to her. She said he left without saying too much more and she just stood there in shock. When her husband came home, she told him what had happened, and he said without hesitation "Call that SOB and tell him to get this car out of my driveway immediately." He knew Joe's history and was concerned for all, especially their young children. She explained she had no way of contacting him, but he did promise to pick it up in a couple of days. He threatened to call the police and have it towed away, but my sister, out of fear of Joe, begged him not to.

Three days later he returned. She said Joe didn't say much to her, just asked her if she'd messed with the car or attempted to get into the trunk, and she assured him she hadn't, but before leaving she told him her husband was furious about the car and the guns being left in their driveway and didn't want him to come back to their house. Her husband didn't want him around her or their children, even threatening to call the police if he returned. His last words to her were to "Fuck off," then he slammed the door and left, taking the car of course.

This vehicle was ultimately the one used in the mass killings near Quartzite, Ariz., later in the year by Gary and his gang.

After his escape, Gary, Randy, and Gary's three sons' geographical route covered several different states. They were all over the place, with no plan. Gary was obviously just desperately running from one place to another, trying to find someone to help them, another vehicle, and sup-plies, and it became clear to his sons that he would hurt anyone who got into his way. According to Ricky and Ray's statements after they were apprehended. Gary had prom-ised them they would go directly to Mexico after the escape, have their mother join them, and live happily ever after. I don't believe that was ever his plan; unfortunately, his sons believed whatever he told them. Over the years, and all those weekly visits to the prison with their mother, they weren't allowed to think for themselves, only what Gary and Dorothy perceived and told them, never allowing them to have thoughts of their own. They had no idea what a sociopath he was until they broke him out of prison and saw him mow down innocent people, anyone who got into his way.

His sons stated in interviews after their capture that they were terrified of him during the entire time they were on the run and insisted they didn't know how to get away from him. I was hesitant to believe this in my heart, as they were all armed. At any time, especially after the first murders, they could have turned their guns on Gary and Randy to prevent any more innocent people from being murdered and run, even to Mexico if that was what they chose, or turn themselves in and pleaded on the mercy of the courts or even turned the guns on themselves. If they were as frightened, as they said in their statements, they had options but chose to stay with Gary and continue this murdering rampage. My thoughts over the years have always been, Donnie Joe as a trained Marine, could have gotten himself and the other two boys away from Gary and Randy, but for some reason, he did not. Was he that afraid of Gary, was where my thoughts lingered and still do?

These boys had such a pathological family environment growing up and braining washing by their mother and Gary on those weekly visits to the prison for as long as they could remember, most of their entire lives. Gary and Dorothy both had strong influences on all boys, except Donnie Joe. At some point, he started making moral decisions for himself and realized the truth about his parents and attempted to do right as he got older and started making plans for his own future. The boys did not grow up as normal children, however dragged to the prison for those weekly visits and consistently told Gary had been railroaded on any/all charges against him each time he was convicted. After the escape, I grieved deeply for Donnie Joe and kept wondering why, why he got involved, he knew better and was vehemently against this idea. My thoughts were confirmed by Ricky and Raymond after they were captured. They told a Detective Donnie Joe only went at the last minute to make sure they didn't get hurt and pulled it off. His love for his brothers was that strong and it ultimately it cost him his life.

The prison guards were familiar with all three boys, as they had been coming to the prison weekly with their mother for most of their lives. The guards as always were friendly and receptive to them, one even asking them why their mother wasn't with them. They explained she would be coming later. They had boxes of food and beverages, which they always brought, as it was allowed in the minimum-security area. Knowing the boys so well and seeing them each Sunday, they didn't check the boxes as well as they should have. They lifted a couple things, then told the boys to go on through. Had the guards searched the boxes more thoroughly, they would have found all the guns on the bottom, underneath all the food items.

As they had already planned, when the guards told them to go on through Randy came out of the control room, and Gary lunged toward the guard shack. The boys pulled the guns out of the boxes, giving one to Gary and one to Randy and they locked all personnel into a closet, giving them time to escape before alarms were set off.

Right after leaving the prison, they immediately switched vehicles. The boys had stashed the Lincoln in the county hospital parking lot over on Adamsville Road just west of Florence. There were so many vehicles in and out of the place, they decided nobody would even notice it. Correctly assuming this, as it days before anyone realized the Ford, they had escaped in had been sitting in the parking lot all along. The prison guards were all tied up and kept in a supply room during the escape, therefore they had plenty of time to get to the hospital parking lot, retrieve the Lincoln and leave the green Ford they had used for the escape. According to Ricky and Raymond's statements after being captured, they went from Florence to Gila Bend, Hyder, Yuma, Quartzsite, Prescott, Ash Fork, Williams, Flagstaff, St. Johns, and on into New Mexico and ultimately Colorado. Another brother, Larry, lived in Flagstaff, however, according to the boy's statements, they made no contact with Larry while in Flagstaff although he owned and operated a gas station right on the main highway. He would have been easy to find, but apparently, they didn't know about the gas station or even perhaps that he lived in Flagstaff.

There was a female friend of Randy's who assisted them in obtaining another vehicle while in Flagstaff, she was later charged with conspiracy and aiding felons in a man hunt, but for some unknown reason, received only probation rather than prison time for her obtaining them another vehicle. According to her statement, she didn't listen to the news, or have any knowledge Randy had escaped, only assisted him due to their long-time friendship. She even went to the bank and borrowed money to purchase another vehicle for him without asking any questions about repayment, etc., or at least, that was her story. She delivered papers for a living and would have had to live in a cave not to have heard this headline news, however she insisted she didn't, even though according to statements, the gang was hiding in her home when a deputy knocked on the door after the visiting logs were checked and law enforcement realized she knew and visited Randy. Gary, Randy and two of the boys were hiding inside her mobile home when a deputy knocked on the door. According to statements made later, the gang decided not to shoot the deputy who came to her door unless he forced his way in, just to stay quiet until he left. That officer was a lucky man that day, as he turned and walked away when nobody answered, unaware that the majority of the Tison Gang was inside, just steps away from him.

There was a man named Bob Adams who was a cell mate of Gary's in earlier years, and they kept in contact with Dorothy through him. Gary was calling Bob, who relayed everything to Dorothy after the escape, about where they were and whatever plans they might have, although it didn't appear, they really had a plan, just desperate criminals running from the law. The boys told officers that both Gary and Dorothy assumed nobody was watching this Bob Adams or tapping his telephone and felt it was safe to communicate. He and Dorothy would communicate directly, in person after Gary would call him. Even with all the surveillance of our family members during the eleven days of the escape, Bob Adams and Dorothy were able to meet on numerous occasions without it raising any red flags for law enforcement, which after the fact, gave reason to believe they weren't watching Dorothy as well as I thought they might.

Finally, out of desperation, Gary called Joe directly at his home and said he needed an airplane to fly them into Mexico and where could they meet. According to Joe's wife, he told him to get him an airplane or his whole family would die. What Gary didn't know was that Joe had already contacted Dave Harrington, Detective at the Pinal County Sheriff's Office and they had tapped his phone. There were undercover officers all around Joe's hidden county home, and they had hoped Gary would show up there so they could arrest him and his gang since he made it clear he wanted to kill Joe. Joe tried to lure him there by telling him he had a nice-sized plane nearby, but Gary didn't trust him. Dave and Joe grew up together, obviously taking different paths in life, but were best of friends as teenagers and continued their friendship well into adulthood. Joe once boasted that he got to see Dave often due to his criminal activity. Damn, what an unhealthy thought process and one hell of a way to have to connect with an old friend. Even knowing Joe's history with the cartel, and knowing he was already under scrutiny, Dave protected Joe and his family well during the time Gary was on the loose terrorizing any and everyone. He went as far as to place them in protective custody in a resort hotel in the Phoenix area.

In hopes of capturing Gary and his gang, Joe and Dave planned and agreed to provide an airplane and fly them into Mexico but he would have to meet him in Clovis, New Mexico, at an old, abandoned runway west of town. Even though Gary never trusted Joe and even less now, he had no idea law enforcement was heavily involved in this plan. Joe told Gary he'd need a couple days to obtain an airplane and Gary had no choice but to agree, as he had nobody else, he could call on. Gary told him he could find the airstrip but told Joe he'd better be there alone or again promised to kill his entire family if he double crossed him. Joe said he understood and would be there.

What Joe really needed was time for Dave to listen to the taped conversation and arrange for them to be in Clovis within a couple days. DPS provided the airplane to fly Dave, Joe, Sgt. Stanford of CGPD, and DPS officers to Clovis. A prop airplane was placed on the old, abandoned runway for Gary to see with Joe visible in the cockpit to anyone who might be looking. Gary contacted Joe once again before he left Casa Grande and Joe told him he could only get a small plane and only had room for himself as the pilot and two passengers. He told Gary the boys couldn't go; he only had room for him and Randy. He explained the boys could turn themselves in, and they would go easier on them, which we all know was crap, but Joe was desperate to draw Gary to that runway in Clovis so he could be arrested. Gary was willing to leave his boys behind to face the music and allow only himself and Randy to fly to Mexico after Joe had told him there was only room for two passengers in the plane. What a dad!

What happened next was unexpected to all those involved. A deputy sheriff of Coconino County told a news reporter in confidence about the arranged meet, and they were finally going to capture the Tison Gang and promised a full story after the fact to this reporter. Apparently, this reporter didn't want to wait and went public with the information. When Gary arrived the Clovis Airport, the place was swarming with news media, although all law enforcement folks were well-hidden. It took the detectives awhile before they knew how the news media knew of this meeting. The deputy sheriff who had revealed this meeting was severely reprimanded for revealing this meeting.

Sgt. Stanford had shared with me when returning that they all felt they were so close to capturing him and put an end to this horrific manhunt. He also elaborated that Gary was more desperate and dangerous now and to use extreme caution for myself and kids. Gary knew when he got close to this abandoned airstrip that Joe had betrayed him, he couldn't see law enforcement, but the place was crawling with news media trucks, so he knew. The boy's statements after capture was that Gary was extremely upset with Joe and his words consistently were "I'm going to kill that SOB and his family for betraying me." He reiterated this over and over according to the boys' statements. It was strongly believed and later confirmed by the boys that Gary's main purpose in coming back to Casa Grande was to kill Joe for his betrayal. However, what he didn't know was Joe and his family were safely tucked away in a resort in Phoenix in protective custody thanks to his friend, Dave. According to sworn statements by Ricky and Raymond after they were captured, they did get close enough to Joe's country home to see that it was swarming with officers hidden in bushes and even inside. It was at this time, they decided to go on into Mexico using the Chuichu Highway. that is often traveled by those visiting Mexico.

I was made aware of this arranged meet in Clovis, New Mexico, by Sgt. Stanford early in the morning before they left. He wanted me to know Gary and his gang were far away, not in this area, and at the present, we were in no danger and could take a breath, but the turmoil remained within the southwestern parts of the country. Sgt. Stanford was truly a good friend and went out of his way keeping me informed and this time by letting me know they were headed to New Mexico. This was his whole reason for telling me as he knew I was terrified that Gary or his boys would show up, and we knew we were in as much danger as anyone might be with them. He assured me this would all be over soon as they were finally going to capture Gary and his gang. He made me promise not to say anything to anyone about this, which I didn't, I took a vow of silence based on our friendship, I was just grateful to know Gary wasn't in this immediate area any longer. or at least currently.

They used a green Ford for the escape from the prison, like what I was driving, which is why I was stopped that Sunday morning with my son. They left that vehicle in the parking lot of Florence Hospital and switched to the Lincoln that the boys has stashed in the lot, the Lincoln that Joe had given them, and they had kept in storage in Phoenix for months. Instead of heading to Mexico, as Gary had promised his sons they would do, they for some unknown reason headed west to Gila Bend, Yuma, and ultimately Quartzite where the Lyons family was found dead a few days later.

I laid in bed in the early morning hours of Aug. 4 listening to the news and heard a family had been found dead in the desert near Quartzite. The news said bodies were found inside a bullet-ridden white Lincoln, one body outside the vehicle, and another victim in the backseat along with a small child. I got physically sick after hearing this on the news; I couldn't quit throwing up, and my legs were weak, I had a strong suspicion this was the Lincoln that Joe had given to Dorothy and Gary's boys. This still haunts everyone who gives it thought even after more than forty years.

I had the business card of an FBI Agent Eschslinger who had interviewed me a few days earlier. He had contacted me through Sgt. Stanford, who had forewarned me he didn't like or trust this agent and to be cautious of him even though I was in no way involved in this horrific ordeal. He was concerned this FBI agent was going to try to make a name for himself with this escape and be a hero and didn't care who he hurt or used in the process, so he warned me too just be cautious when around him. I wasn't the least bit impressed with him professionally or personally. When I did finally agree to meet with him after numerous phone calls to me, he appeared far more concerned about getting with me rather than doing police work, even going so far as to ask if he could see me socially after this was all over. I was appalled at the suggestion and felt he was using his position as an FBI agent to harass me. Everything about this entire situation was awkward, threatening, and embarrassing as they were still those who thought because Gary was our brother, we would help him, and we were all like him. Nothing could have been further from the truth ... we were terrified of him as children/youth and even more so now. I assured him that if I heard anything, I would contact him, thinking at the time, I would probably never call him, as he came across as an arrogant man who thought because he was an FBI agent, I'd jump right into bed with him.

After listening to the news, I tried to call Sgt. Stanford but was unable to reach him so I found this FBI agent's business card and called him. I asked him if he knew anyone on the scene of this horrible crime scene near Quartzite, and he said he did. I asked him to have someone scratch this vehicle and see if it was purple colored underneath. He asked me why, and I yelled, "Just fucking do it and call me back!" He called back within a matter of moments and said the Lincoln was purple underneath. I told him this was possibly the car that Joe had given to Dorothy and her sons and that this was most likely the work of Gary and his gang.

He asked if he could pick me up and fly me to the scene to ascertain if this was the same vehicle. I said, "Absolutely not," that I had never seen the vehicle, only knew of its existence because of my sister, and there was absolutely no way I was going to go look at something so horrible and that I was already physically sick just hearing about it. At that point he threatened to have me arrested for conspiracy, became arrogant again, and demanding. I said, "Conspiracy to what, you ass? I only called and told you this because my family and I want him caught more than anyone as we are terrified, and I remember my sister telling me about this Lincoln." I explained to him that I called him hoping that if this was Gary and his gang, they could ascertain what type of vehicle they were now driving and hopefully prevent anyone else from being hurt or killed. I assured him my next call was to Sgt. Stanford at CGPD to let him know how he was harassing me. He told me that wouldn't be necessary and apologized for threatening me. He apparently knew of Sgt. Stanford's reputation, as a quiet, yet powerful man, easily angered, and tough as nails. I let him know I was calling Sgt. Stanford anyway as at this point, I didn't trust anyone except him and our Sheriff. I later learned that Sgt. Stanford had called him and told him about any communication with me from this point on would go through him, that he wasn't to contact me again for any reason.

According to Ricky's narrative of what occurred during the 11 days they were on the loose, they needed to get another vehicle. Gary didn't trust Joe and guessed he probably had told law enforcement about the Lincoln once they had escaped, and it all got so crazy. He was right; Joe did so to save himself, but Gary apparently only thought he might at this point, according to Ricky, he didn't know for sure.

The horrific and ultimate death of the Lyons family started when Gary decided they needed to switch vehicles, not being sure Joe had not already told law enforcement about the Lincoln. Having a flat tire on the Lincoln forced that decision. All this planning and the dumb bastards didn't have a spare tire. Ricky stated that Gary told Ray to go stand on the side of the road near Quartzite and stop someone while they all hid in the bushes. Ray was young and had a kind face; anyone would have stopped to help him as he looked like a kid. Unfortunately for this young Marine and his family, they stopped to assist what they thought was a young man in distress, little did they know, the notorious Tison gang was hidden in the shrubs a few feet away. As soon as the young man got out of his car, the others ran up to him and his family from the bushes. Gary and Randy shot this entire family, including a baby, and it was overwhelmingly devastating to everyone that heard of it and still is. They took their car and continued their rampage. At this point, according to Ricky's statement, they were terrified of Gary, as they knew if they ran, he would kill them too. All three boys discussed running, but after killing the family outside of Quartzite, Gary watched them closely, as he knew they were scared and wanted to bolt, according to Ricky's statement after their capture. Gary had openly stated on numerous occasions that he would kill anyone who got in his way. According to the boys' statements, they were absolutely terrified of Gary from that point on. They have always idolized him and honestly thought he was a good man who had been railroaded all those times he spent in prison, because of their parents' brainwashing over the years that never allowed them to form their own opinions. As Donnie Joe got older, his visits to the prison became far and few between. He began to slowly see his father for what he was and wanted a better life for himself; he decided to stay away from the prison completely until his mother would put extreme pressure on him to go visit Gary. From transcripts I learned that he tried talking his mother and brothers out of helping Gary escape right down to the day prior. Donnie had told his mother that Gary had done the crimes and should do the time, but they wouldn't hear of it. He even went to so far as to tell his mother that Gary had never been railroaded on any of his charges over the years, that he had done his own research and learned the truth about Gary, that he consistently broke the law, served time, and was now planning an escape that would probably get them all killed. I always will believe that he went with Ricky and Raymond to assist in the escape to prevent their mother from going with them and because he wanted to protect his brothers and felt they couldn't pull this off without him. Of course, he too thought once they got Gary out, they would go right to Mexico without anyone being hurt, not realizing until it was too late what a sociopath his dad was.

Ricky stated that Gary told them he was going to leave the Lyons family water and supplies in the desert after they took them off the main highway back into the desert, and by the time they got help, they would be far into Mexico, and they would already have another car by then so they wouldn't be connected to the Lyons car. He had sent the boys away, but when they heard the gunshots, they knew Gary and Randy had killed them.

Ricky said Gary swore to them it was Randy and not him that killed this family, but they knew in their hearts at that point their father was a sociopathic hardened criminal with no conscience and desperate as hell. All those years, their mother had dragged them to the prison to visit their dad, they never saw this side of him, as he kept it well-hidden from them knowing he and Dorothy's ultimate plan was to use the boys to help him escape.

On August 4, Game Warden Peoples noticed a vehicle in

the shrubs and got out to investigate. He found the bodies of the Lyons, except for the young niece, Terri Jo. They had all been shot with a rifle.

As sickening and unbelievable as this all was, after this all came out, one of the victims last name was Tyson and this all occurred a few yards from Tyson Wash. I laid awake at night for weeks wondering why this had happened to such a beautiful family, who only stopped to help what they thought was a young man who needed assistance on the side of the road. It cost them their lives and the life of their infant son and niece Terri Jo, who was only 16 years old. Jo Ann Tyson, Terri Jo's mother, testified in court sometime later that she had woke during the night to hear her daughter call out "Mommy," as she died in the desert from a shotgun blast. She stated it was clear as day; she even went into her room and sat on her bed. She knew in her heart something bad had happened to her daughter but was unable to reach them or other relatives by phone. Terri Jo's body and the bodies of the young married couple in Colorado had still not been located when the funeral was held for the Lyon's family in Omaha, Neb., the same day as the Roadblock on Chui Chu Highway where Rick, Ray and Randy were captured, Donnie Joe killed, and Gary went missing in the desert.

Governor Babbitt authorized a Cooperative Investigation Team of several agencies, in several counties, putting Tom Brawley in charge to head up this team. Tom Brawley had a reputation of being a hardworking and ruthless lawman who vowed to get the job done ... His promise to our governor was that he would capture the Tison Gang one way or another. They combed the desert once again for

Terri Jo's body. She had placed her dog's tags on her wrist so her remains could be identified. She knew she was going to die in that hot desert, alone and a shot gun blast to her lower back. She had managed to crawl several yards away and get herself under some shrubs, as her dog laid next to her.

The Judges were a young married couple, honeymooning in Colorado. They were unfortunate enough to be targeted by the Tison Gang for their vehicle, the van that was ultimately in the roadblock capture. Had it not been for the van, their families may have never known what happened to them or where they were buried. The Judge's bodies in Colorado were not found until a couple of months later in November. Ricky and Ray had disclosed the location of their graves after their attorney's attempted to get a plea deal to take the death penalty off the table. Only then did they disclose.

In 1979, Joe was charged with Conspiracy to Gary's escape and received only four years. At that time, he was serving time for in a Federal Prison for a drug-related charge. The judge ordered he serve his four years for Conspiracy concurrently with the time he was already serving. He was paroled in 1982.

The only time I had seen Joe in years was one night I was cooking dinner and Frank said, "Lynda, isn't that your brother on the news?" He stood on the Federal courthouse steps in Tucson, being interviewed and said, "I'm no different than any other businessman, except periodically, I have to serve time." Just when you thought it couldn't get worse ... one of them brought additional shame to us all, such as Joe's comment on the evening news.

The adage "Live by example" took new meaning for me growing up. I never had any desire to break the law, make any fast money or do anything that would endanger my freedom or put my family in jeopardy. I had several examples in my entire life of how *crime does not pay.*

Chapter 17
Terror Continues
with Gary and His Gang
on the Loose

Nobody can possibly imagine the terror in the Southwestern part of the U.S. Folks who normally didn't carry guns, were now armed, everyone was afraid. My family as much, if not more, than anyone else.

I kept my mother as close as I possibly could, as she was withdrawn, depressed, and wouldn't leave her home, not even to go to church, even though church and her faith were a big part of her life. She had told me that people kept quietly asking her questions about Gary and the boys, as though she knew something that wasn't headline news. She never gossiped, no matter what. She always told us girls if we had a problem with someone or heard something about another person that it was our duty to take them to God in prayer and not tell others what we knew or heard about them. With so many folks trying to corner her before, after or even during church for inside info/gossip, she simply quit going and wouldn't even answer the door unless it was one of us girls.

As each day passed, it became more dramatic and terrifying. My sole purpose was to protect my mother and children as much as I possibly could; unfortunately, that was all anyone talked about it and even at the La Grande Pool my kids were approached by not only noisy folks but news reporters as well. I no longer let them go on their own, but either swam with them or sat on a bench making sure news reporters didn't come near them.

On the morning of Aug. 11, I was in bed listening to the early morning radio news, way before dawn. It came across that there had been a shoot-out at a roadblock south on Chui Chu Road and was believed to be with the Tison Gang. Dear Lord, perhaps they had finally been captured was my immediate thought, but then I immediately thought of mother and whether she was listening to the news. I immediately called my friend Sharon to take my kids and went to mother's. She had not turned on the TV yet, and as we had a cup of coffee, I explained to her what I'd heard about the roadblock and reassured her we would watch the news together and ask God to protect innocent folks. That was all that was on the news, on every channel.

According to records, the only reason the roadblock had been set up on Chui Chu Highway south of Casa Grande was due to an armory being broken to in Gila Bend. Law enforcement had already found the Lyons' family dead in the desert and had connected the Lincoln to the Tison Gang and assumed the break-in of the armory was for more guns and ammunition. They figured they would head to Mexico, and this was one of the most traveled routes. Gary had a history of breaking into an armory here in Casa Grande in 1961 and left with a trunk load of guns and ammunition that he sold in Mexico. As it turned out, they were not the ones who broke into the armory, but it was a good call on behalf of the Sheriff and Dave Herrington to set up the roadblock, as Gary ultimately did run right into it.

What officials didn't know was that Gary had made one last call to our brother-in-law, who had a plane to fly them into Mexico. My brother-in-law's quick response was to tell Gary that he couldn't get a plane off the ground even he wanted to, as we were all under constant surveillance and would be stopped immediately if he attempted to take off. The call came as a surprise, but he reacted quickly to avoid telling Gary anything that would set him off. Apparently, Gary slammed the phone down and made the decision to use the van they had stolen in Colorado to make a run for the border, coincidently shortly after the armory in Gila Bend was robbed.

The state alert for roadblocks had been called off late into the night, however Dave Harrington knew Gary would come back to Casa Grande at some point, as he always did when he had escaped, and he also had a score to settle with Joe for double crossing him in New Mexico. Dave's strong belief that he was in the area and was going to wait and keep these roadblocks in Pinal County active, specifically roads heading to Mexico, near Joe's house. He was working strictly off a gut instinct, as he told me months later. He reminded me his instincts were generally right, and they got them ... well, everyone but Gary who apparently ran from the wrecked van yelling "Every man for himself!" after the shoot-out at the second roadblock. Wow! What a guy! Can any father imagine leaving their sons to face the music for the chaos that he had created? It was as I told Dorothy years prior ... he was for himself and nobody else. His family finally realized this ... but much too late.

News helicopter pictures were shown of the silver and

blue late model van they were captured in. I didn't know who that van belonged to or where it had been stolen from but knew in my heart Gary and his gang probably had killed probably killed owners. The Sheriff's Department ran the license plates of the van, and it belonged to James and Margene Judge, a newlywed couple from Texas who were honeymooning in Colorado. Their families were worried sick, as they had not heard from them since Aug. 8, however nobody linked them to the Tison Gang until the roadblock and the van was identified. When this information was reported on the news, I immediately went to St. Anthony's Church, lit a candle, and prayed for the Judge's souls, as I knew in my heart, they were dead. Their bodies weren't discovered until November 1978 when Ricky and Ray's attorneys used it as a bargaining chip to remove the death sentence off the table for them both. I went for a long ride alone after hearing this as I was distraught that these two would not give the victims' families the decency to locate their loved ones and give them a decent burial unless it was too their advantage to do so.

My thoughts drifted to the contempt I felt for Federal Judge Mueche, who had declared the death penalty unconstitutional in Arizona years prior. If not for this, seven people would be alive. I could not voice my opinion around my mother, but had this Federal judge not declared the death penalty unconstitutional, Gary would have been executed for the prison guards' death many years prior, six innocent people would be alive, and his son, Donnie Joe would have lived and gone onto make something of his life, and his other two sons wouldn't be spending life in prison.

As mother and I watched the news, every detail, true or

not, was being discussed. One station showed a view from a helicopter and reported an ambulance was standing by a quarter mile away to attend to the driver who had been shot but wasn't allowed entry due to Gary not being in custody. They at this time had Randy, Ricky, and Ray in custody, but Gary had run into the desert. The helicopter shots were showing them each lying in the back of sheriff's trucks with a blanket spread over them after they had been stripped. It became apparent to both mother and I that Donnie Joe was the one who was driving and had been shot. There was absolutely no color to mother's face, and she sat quietly next to me, praying, and asking God to protect all involved, not just her kin, for that is who she was, compassionate and caring. She squeezed my hand and said, "I pray they find Gary before he hurts anyone else, especially those deputies out there looking for him." Then as I thought she was just speaking to herself, however out loud, she said "Gary has done so much wrong since he left the church at 15, and I always thought he would have been a preacher, not a criminal. I should have left RC when Gary and Joe asked me to when they were young. They told me they would work and take care of all of us if I would just leave RC. I should have done that because he was a bad influence and made them what they are." She also added that if RC had not had so much control over her boys, "they would have turned out completely different as you girls had." This was the first time she had ever admitted that RC was wrong, a bad influence and that she should have left him years ago and taken her children with her. I honestly never thought I would see the day she would say that...but what was and had been going on was horrific and innocent people had died at the hands of her son. She spoke, looking at nothing, and felt she was speaking her thoughts out loud. She kept saying "it was her fault because she stayed with RC".

After what seemed like hours of sitting quietly watching the news, mother told me how Gary was originally a God-fearing man, who sang in church, taught youth groups, and was an integral member of the church they attended in Lamont Cotton Camp outside of Arvin, California. She apparently felt the need to say all of this out loud, I could tell it had been on her heart for some time, perhaps since Gary and Joe's first criminal act at the young age of 16, but she never verbalized it until this day. We kept being interrupted, as her phone kept ringing and I was appalled at how many of those good ol' church folks asked me if we had seen the news. Really!? Before leaving, I unplugged the phone and told mother it was best for her, she agreed.

My friend Sharon, who was taking care of my children, called to say the boys had watched the news downstairs at a friend's house and were quite upset realizing Donnie Joe had been shot. I did not want to leave mother but knew I had to go pick up my kids. When I returned with them, the news was showing grisly crimson photographs of Donnie Joe's body from a helicopter, and I decided no more news. I turned the TV off and wasn't sure, but knew I had to somehow explain this to my children who had been traumatized. Afterwards, mother and I cooked lunch, turned cartoons on the TV and tried to get through this ordeal together and with my children. mother played dominos with the kids, as I cleaned the kitchen. Later I decided to take the kids to La Grande Pool, watch them swim, and mother had promised to take a nap.

To my surprise, numerous youths in the pool were aware of the roadblock, the shooting, and all details covered by every news station. They started making fun of my boys, calling them names, and asking the lifeguard to make them get out of the pool. Dear Lord .... It was one thing that I had to endure this from the public all these years due to the criminal activity of my father and brothers, but another thing altogether when it came to my kids. At this point, I wasn't sure where we were going to go or what we were going to do, but I knew I had to do everything I could to protect them. I tried to explain to them while swinging in the park that sometimes people can be cruel and that none of this was in anyway their fault and that I would protect them, although I knew in my heart it was going to be impossible to protect them from public scrutiny, even other children.

As school resumed in September, another reminder that I couldn't completely protect my boys from this as they entered Jr. High School, DeAnna was still incredibly young and wasn't subjected to what the boys were. One boy, whom I won't name, brought colored pictures to school to pass along to others of Donnie Joe's body, showing his head was partially blown off. When it came to the attention of the principal, he called and suggested I pick up the boys after they were shown the pictures. They were obviously extremely upset on so many levels it couldn't even be described. While in the principal's office, with the boys in an adjoining room, I asked him who the boy was. He informed me his father worked for the county attorney's office and that he had apparently brought these pictures home from work. It wasn't clear yet if he gave them to his son or that his son stole them from his briefcase. However, the damage was done, and one of my sons had nightmares for weeks after that. We didn't have homeschooling at the time, or I would surely have removed them. I just continually talked to them about what had happened and what they saw, and that it was a time for them to be as brave as possible, hold their heads up high, and utterly understand this was in no way their fault ... any of it. It was exactly what my mother had told me since early childhood. I set up therapy appointments, but I knew nothing was going to take away this nightmare for them and my sons, and seriously considered relocating to another city.

My friend Tim had offered to buy me a house in the Phoenix area, to get lost in the crowded city where nobody would know who we are or that we were related to this monster. Unfortunately, I explained to him that with three kids, one of them would tell someone, and they would tell someone, and we would have to deal with it all over again. At least here, a lot of folks knew me and my children and knew us to be of good character. I simply was not up to this risk of starting over and trying to explain how this murder was my brother. I graciously thanked him for caring but that I would stay here in Casa Grande, right in the house he had purchased for me and the kids when our apartment was broken into, and after he had to move us there from the Francisco Grande earlier.

The Lyon's family was having a funeral in Omaha for their family the same day of the capture at the roadblock. As I learned later, it was a full military funeral with the child being buried in the mother's arms. My family and I grieved as to how this precious family had died and shared the grief of the surviving family. They died only because they were kind and saw a young boy needing help on the side of the road they stop to help. However, Terri Jo's body still had not been located. I can only assume the questioning of the remaining fugitives consisted of ascertaining where her body and the owners of the van they had stolen was, assuming they too had been killed.

Frequent headline news that the State of Arizona Assistant Attorney General Schafter and Governor Babbitt placed Tom Brawley the authority to head up a team called Arizona Cooperative Investigation Team to investigate everything from the day of the escape to the Tison Gang's capture, those who assisted them and those who died at their hands. The news reported since this investigation covered so many different counties and states, it needed a formal team to investigate and with full jurisdiction in all counties and states, they wanted no mistakes in prosecution of these criminals. From what I had read, Tom Brawley, an experienced, determined and harden lieutenant with Coconino County Sheriff's Department was just the man to handle this investigation.

Chapter 18
Donnie Joe, Gary,
and Joe's Funerals

Donnie Joe was pronounced death at the scene of the roadblock when the medics were finally allowed, hours later, to enter and remove his body. He was taken to a forensic lab for an autopsy and eventually his body was released to Cole & Maud Funeral Home here in Casa Grande.

I could not share my feelings with family members, especially my mother, however I was almost relieved that Donnie Joe had not survived this nightmare, as I knew he would remain in prison for the rest of his life, and he was just way too full of life to do that. I always will believe he was pressured into this a day prior to the escape by his mother, who didn't feel her other two boys could pull it off. I knew he would have eventually taken his own life, and I had such mixed feelings about his death at the roadblock and why he hadn't turned his gun on Gary and Randy and stopped this insanity before it got this far. My thoughts consistently drifted back to Donnie Joe's military training, as he surely could have taken Gary and Randy out at any time. Ricky and Raymond's testimony indicated they were all armed. What the hell was he thinking? Why didn't he? I suppose I'll never know.

Shortly after Donnie Joe's body had been released, I started hearing rumors of the calls and threats being received by the local funeral home. Local folks didn't want them to handle the funeral or be buried in Mountain View Cemetery and made it abundantly clear.

Steve Foster, one of the sons of Cole & Maud Funeral Home and the only funeral home in the area at the time, had been a good friend over the years, so I reached out to him. He asked me to stop by, and we went for a walk over to Elliott Park where I'd spent a great deal of time as a child. He confirmed the threats that he and his family were receiving to handle the funeral and the fact that Dorothy had paid for two lots at the cemetery in the veteran's section was only fueling the fire. Small town and all, news traveled fast, and by the time I met with Steve, it was pretty much all over Casa Grande. I gave him an out and told him I'd understand completely if he refused and wanted to turn the body over to another funeral home, preferably in Phoenix or Tucson, and would explain to my family why. He assured me his family was professionals and didn't judge anyone, it wasn't their place. His place he stated, "was to bury those who had passed in whatever fashion the family wanted and was willing to pay for." Donnie Joe having been in the Marines entitled him to be buried in the veteran's section, but I could honestly understand how others would feel differently about this considering their loved ones who had served, were also buried in this same area.

Steve told me that Dorothy had provided Donnie Joe's military forms, and he was entitled to be buried there, however her purchasing the second lot, which obviously was for Gary, is what stirred up even more controversy. He assured me that nothing would come of this and thanked me for my concern for his business and his family. I thanked him, hugged him, and apologized that they had been subject to this. Donnie Joe's funeral was held nine days prior to Gary's remains being located. The funeral home and cemetery were surrounded with cops, as they felt if Gary was still alive or anywhere close, he would try to view the funeral from a distance. Of course, we later learned he had been dead for days; however, nobody knew this as the time of funeral. So, every precaution by law enforcement was being taken.

I had told my mother I would pick her up and take her to the funeral, then onto the cemetery. When I arrived, she informed me that Dorothy had called her earlier and wanted to ride with us. Holy shit! As I've mentioned before, never say it can't get worse in this family because it always did in some way or another. Since mother had already told Dorothy we would pick her up, there wasn't much I could do about it except to hope for the best with all the reporters I knew would be there.

When we arrived at the funeral home, a news reporter soon realized I had both the wife and mother of Gary in my car, and the media literally encapsulated the vehicle. We had the same situation at the cemetery, so I told mother and Dorothy to stay in the car and got out to speak to some of them, asking them to please back away and let this grandmother lay her Grandson to rest ... despite who he was and what they had done. The response was appalling, and some of the language, even I hadn't heard before. I knew this whole scene was going to be bad, yet I had no idea it would be this bad. I just wanted to protect my mother. There were two law enforcement officers close by, and I gently asked if they could remove these reporters and was shocked at their response. I was told "anything you fucking Tisons' get, you deserved." Oh Lord, I wondered if it was too late to just get back in the car and run away, with or without mother and Dorothy.

Before I could even get the door back open to turn off the car and get mother out, Joe released his Doberman dogs, and they almost attacked the reporters. He finally called them off, but the dogs stood on top of the funeral car during the entire graveside service, growling and showing their teeth, bringing even more chaos to what an already bad situation was. This whole funeral, both at the funeral home and cemetery, was a living nightmare. As I stood there at the cemetery, behind my mother, I wondered how in the hell it all came to this. My mind kept drifting to the innocent victims of the Tison Gang, how they had suffered and the loss for their families – all because Gary wanted out of prison – just didn't seem right. I kept thinking I should be feeling something for my family, but it just wasn't there. I'd always been a bit different in my thinking and right now, my thoughts were with the victims even though I was standing at my nephew, Donnie Joe's grave.

Gary's remains were found by a male employee of Papago Chemical Company nine days later, just a mile from the roadblock crash site. To say it was a relief to me was an understatement. I always knew he was somewhere in this area and feared his coming to family for help, so I was terrified for myself, my kids, and other family members.

Gary's funeral was even worse than Donnie Joe's with even more aggressive reporters. I didn't blame them – it was news, and they were just doing their jobs –but they did not realize what innocent family members already had experienced at no fault of their own and now going to be exposed again and prosecuted on the evening news. Fortunately for me, I only had my mother with me this time. Dorothy had ridden with my sister and other family members. Mother's minister did the graveside service, which was probably an extremely difficult one to do. What could he possibly say about this sociopathic killer who had taken six innocent peoples' lives and left his own son to die in the van at the roadblock after being shot? The service was extremely short, and his only comments were "Gary Tison, rest in peace in the hands of a just God." That was about it except for comfort for mother and prayers for the family. He ended in prayer, and we got up to leave .... and surely not soon enough for me. I wanted to go home and hide but most importantly, I wanted my mother home safe as none of us knew what to expect next.

A lot of spectators surrounding the cemetery and Steve said they had received even more threats since learning Gary was going to be buried next to Donnie Joe. One he shared even said they were going to dig them both up after the service and burn them outside the cemetery. I never shared this with my mother, only my sisters as mother simply couldn't handle anymore. She did mention on the ride home that she saw men holding shovels near the gravesite and I passed it off as the men who worked at the cemetery and luckily for me, she didn't question it. I was told by the sheriff that he had men who were standing by to make sure this didn't happen and had told the men who made this threat that it was a serious crime to dig up bodies, not to mention burning them. Apparently, they took heed and decided not to carry through with their threat.

Of course, it was all over every news station and regular scheduled programs were even being interrupted to carry the funeral of Gary live. I encouraged mother to leave the TV off and rest. I picked up some food for her on the way home. My kids were with Sharon, and I needed to pick them up and make sure they hadn't watched any of this on TV.

Though Randy, Ricky and Raymond were in custody, Donnie Joe and Gary were dead and buried but, in my heart, I knew this was far from over. People were not going to soon forget and understandable so. Afterall, it wasn't us who had committed these autarchies crimes, unfortunately for us, many had believed the family was "guilty by relationship."

The days and weeks that continued didn't ease the burden for any of us. Two of my sisters went home to Tulsa, Martha lived in Maricopa, and I felt they were all protected, however here I was with three kids and needed to work. The question was...who would the hell hire me now!?

The Courts had appointed Michael Beers and Harry Bagnall to represent Ricky and Raymond ... now more front-page news for the family to have to deal with. The Pinal County trials for the escape and the Yuma County trials for the death of the Lyons family were to start in January 1979. The prosecuting attorney in Yuma County had approved a plea agreement to avoid the death penalty if they would tell where the couple in Colorado were buried, as it was strongly assumed, they were dead. This young couple were on their honeymoon in Colorado when they were accosted by Gary and his gang, who killed them and took their van. Also, they would have to give details of their mother's involvement. Judge Keddie of Yuma County instructed the jury to limit their verdict to First Degree Murder only. He appeared passionate toward the victims, as he should have been. Ricky and Raymond showed little to no remorse for the victims during the trials, both in Pinal and Yuma counties. It made the hairs on the back of one's neck stand up when you would hear how callused they were about the innocent lives lost. I wanted no part of these trials, but mother insisted on going. I did agree to take her to the Pinal County trials after begging her not to go. We were waiting in the outer entrance and had to endure the stares of many whom you could tell wanted to hurt us and surely were disgusted by our presence. I recognized F.H. Davis; the father of the new bride who had been killed in Colorado from seeing him interviewed on the news. He was walking toward us, and I felt so sick to my stomach. Mother didn't recognize him, but I immediately stood in front of her in what I guessed was an attempt to protect her. He walked up to me, offered his handshake, looked around me, introduced himself and said, "Mrs. Tison I am so sorry for everything you have had to endure, and I want you to know that you are in my daily prayers." I was simply overwhelmed with this man's empathy for mother as her son had killed his daughter and new husband after stealing their van in Colorado. Mother started crying and offered her hand and sympathy for the loss of his daughter and husband. Of course, everyone within earshot was listening and trying to get in for a better look, news people were taking pictures, and I knew I had to get out of there and take her with me. I explicitly said, "We don't need to be here, Mother, and we have to go now. I can't do this anymore, and you shouldn't either." She offered no resistance, and we left.

We stopped at restaurant to eat, and it was a nightmare situation with everyone staring and pointing at my mother. One even said loudly "That's Gary Tison's mother." We left and went home to eat. It just reiterated in my mind that this was never going to go away .... at least not in this part of the world, and we would be subject to this type of behavior for possibly years to come. That thought was confirmed over the years to include a front-page newspaper article with pictures as recently as December 8, 2020.

Before the trials started as I was preparing dinner for my kids and I, the news interrupted whatever I was watching to report Ricky had escaped from Pinal County Jail. Oh, absolutely not is all I could think of! This could not possibly be happening again! As I had done so many times prior, I became sick to my stomach and ran to the bathroom to throw up. Afterwards, I showered, told the kids to pack some bags for themselves for a field trip, and off to San Diego we went. I had made the decision to not subject my children to anymore of this Tison BS. I called my friend, Tim, and he said he had already made reservations at a nice hotel in San Diego and tickets were waiting as well for me and the kids to enjoy SeaWorld. Money was limited for me, and Tim knew this, so he made sure, after hearing Ricky had escaped, that we were taken care of, and I will be forever grateful to him for such friendship.

I sat in the hotel lobby while the kids were in the pool so I could listen to the news. I learned Ricky had been captured within a few hours and was grateful. I called Tim, and we chuckled about already being in beautiful San Diego, tickets to SeaWorld, and all other expenses taken care of .... we decided to stay and enjoy, and he agreed wholeheartedly. I knew my kids needed a break and God knows I surely did! As I sat in the lobby watching the news, I overheard some folks commenting about the news and how horrible this escape and capture had been and all the lives lost and being happy they didn't live in Arizona and didn't know this family as they had heard the whole family was bad. Little did they know, Gary's sister was sitting right next to them. I had no intentions of responding, as difficult as it was for me not to comment after they made the statement of "they heard the whole damn family was bad news," but I decided I was in a place where nobody knew me and wanted to keep it that way ... at least for a few days.

Joe died in summer 2014, and I was contacted by his long-time friend and lawyer in Tucson. Joe periodically spoke about his connections both inside and outside of the Federal prison system and with the Cartel and apparently, they were somewhat the truth. He was the only Federal prisoner I had ever heard of who was being treated in the Mayo Clinic in Rochester, Minnesota, in his last days. Most Federal prisoners were treated at a local hospitals or prison infirmaries .... but not Joe. Mayo Clinic it was.

His lawyer called me to tell me he had passed and had requested he be cremated and wanted his ashes scattered near his old home out near the mountain where he and his family had lived for so long, southeast of Casa Grande. He asked if I would be there, and I told him I would. Despite whom he was and what he had done, he was still my brother and I felt I should go. I called my sisters and my daughter, DeAnna, and told them of the time I'd meet with the lawyer at the truck stop on Sunland Gin Road. DeAnna didn't realize what a bad guy Joe had always been, as he was always kind to her. She wasn't aware that he had one of his men threaten to cut up her face years prior if I didn't keep my mouth shut about what had transpired when I had to patch up one of these friends from a gunshot wound. She will only learn this for the first time when reading this book with all the details.

DeAnna contacted a friend of hers who does iron work and asked if he would make a cross for her uncle's final resting place. He agreed to do so, not having any idea who her uncle was. He made it out of friendship to her.

We met the lawyer in the parking lot of Love's Truck Stop, and I introduced my daughter and sisters to him, as I had met him years before when Joe helped with mother's expenses at the nursing home when she first became incompetent due to dementia. He told me he wasn't familiar with the location although he had been to Joe's house on numerous occasions, but it had been years. He asked me to lead, point out Joe's house, and continue until I found a spot for scattering his ashes. I drove slowly down the road with my daughter, the lawyer, and my sisters following behind. Joe's wife and children had moved to Safford, so I heard and I didn't know who lived in the house now, so I didn't stop. As we drove past, I slowed down, pointed out Joe's house and continued, closer to the mountain side. I saw a place a bit off the road, which had a big saguaro growing inside a wash, that seemed like a good spot to scatter ashes, so I maneuver there with all still following. The lawyer was driving what appeared to be an expensive Mercedes and probably wondered if he was starting to wish he hadn't Asked me, but followed along.

We got out, the lawyer with Joe's ashes and DeAnna with

the beautiful cross and headed toward the saguaro. The lawyer opened the box and asked if anyone wanted to say anything after he scattered Joe's ashes. I was conflicted in my own mind but spoke mainly due to love for our mother as this was her son, no matter who and what he'd done, and she wasn't here, as she had passed a few years earlier. I bowed my head, said a prayer, and verbalized my thoughts of "When Joe wasn't being a bad guy, he really was a good guy. He was liked by many and feared by even more". It just sort of came out before I realized I had said it out loud. The lawyer sort of smiled, as I knew he understood, for he had been Joe's friend and lawyer for many years.

Coming prepared with a hammer, DeAnna pounded the large cross in the ground, also said a few words and prayers, and then looked at the lawyer and informed him the cross had been made by a friend of hers who was also a Border Patrol agent who did iron work on the side. The lawyer absolutely doubled up laughing and said "it seems odd but appropriate that the cross for Joe's final resting place would have been made by a Border Patrol agent" considering he ran drugs for years, flying them into the country late at night onto his own landing strip nearby, and having heavy security all around. The lawyer couldn't quit laughing, as he just found this to be amazingly funny, he was still chuckling when he got into his car. I had to explain to my daughter why he found this to be so funny.

I couldn't help but be relieved that at least with this funeral, unlike Donnie Joe's and Gary's, there were no news media, cameras in our faces, or a multiple police presence. I already had asked the lawyer to please not run the obituary in the local newspaper, and he didn't. He ran the obituary in a Tucson newspaper with Joe's alias name of Joseph Aaron and listed no relatives.

He asked that we join him for lunch as he stated he had known Joe for so very many years, but knew little about his family, especially the sisters. We sat for hours, and his main question was "how did you girls turn out so good when obviously all the men in your family were criminals?" We started explaining how our entire lives mother had attempted to shield us from RC's influence. She did the best she could but was so devoted to RC that she allowed us to be raised in an extremely difficult and abusive situation. It was only by the grace of God that we didn't turn out like our father and brothers.

One of the stories I shared with him was about after dinner while growing up in the same household. There was usually a card game going on in the living room, and I've always loved playing cards even though that, too, was against our mother's religion. Once I finished doing dishes and joined in the card game, mother came in, got me, and said she had found food on a fork and made my sister and I drag out every dish and wash them over again. This took hours. I thought at the time she was just a mean old lady, however, I realized later in life that it was her way of keeping us away from RC and the boys by having as little contact as possible with them. That wasn't always easy considering we always lived in small, usually one-bedroom houses.

If she went to hang clothes on the clothesline out back, us girls went and helped. I don't ever remember her leaving me in the house alone with the boys, unless it was necessary. My sisters shared a few stories, and he seemed to be amazed at how pleasant and kind we were.

Chapter 19
Getting into Real Estate

If you think we didn't pay one hell of a price for our father and brother's criminal behaviors over our lifetime, then think again!

I moved ahead professionally as tough as it was enduring the stares, gossip and some just outright asking me if I was Gary's sister. I finally started responding with "Why do you ask?" while looking them straight in the eyes, usually stopping them before going any further.

When I married Frank, my children loved him and he loved them back, however, they all decided they didn't like the idea that we had different last names. I legally changed my middle name to Smith, and they seem to accept this, and we even chuckled about it. By hyphenating my middle name, most assumed when meeting folks for the first time, it was my maiden name, so it often stopped those concerned folks from asking questions I had no desire to answer.

Professionally, for me, it often felt like "two steps forward .... one backwards" or for me, it appeared "one step forward ... two steps back"? Have you ever found yourself in a situation in your life where you looked in the mirror and said to yourself "I made it" despite it all, only to have someone cut you off at the knees? Well, I found myself in that situation .... again, while at a conference in downtown Phoenix during the 1980s.

I obtained a real estate license mainly for the purpose of

investments. I had a few investors who looked for good deals (generally distressed properties they could flip), but unless I invested along with them, which wasn't always the case, the only way for me to make any money was to obtain a license so I could collect part of the commissions being paid by the seller, which is why I originally obtained a real estate license.

I was asked to speak to the top 500 Realtors in Arizona, and it was, without a doubt, the greatest honor I'd ever know. I felt like all my hard work was paying off, despite my history of dealing with the crap we had to clean up from our father and brothers all those years. I grew up ugly and thin and was told on a consistent basis that I wasn't very smart and even told I should learn to be a good cook as it was my only change of getting any kind of man in the future. Well ... nothing like a little motivation for a young girl growing up in an already totally and completely dysfunction environment, with abuse on every level. Once again, as I look back, I realized they were motivating me far more than they realized ... I was going to get an education and "make it" in this mean, nasty and cruel world, despite them.

To this day, I'm still not sure why they asked me to speak at this conference, although I had a good reputation and moved a lot of property, both residential and commercial. They apparently did not know who I was related to when they extended the invitation. I once had an investor at a dinner party tell others, "Lynda's handshake is as good as any contract I ever held." To me, this was quite the reference for future investors, and I had worked hard to earn it.

When meeting with investors, I always made sure they knew who I was related to before entering into a contract.

J.O. Barnes was a local man who became not only an investor but a great friend to both Frank and me. He loved the adventure of investing but once told me, "I don't care how much we make, but if we lose any, you and I are done." Wow! OK! That statement surely kept me focused. I had heard through the grapevine that he was a serious investor, so I contacted him to ask for a breakfast meeting to pitch an investment property. I shared the portfolio with him and asked him to please go over it at his convenience and call me after, which he promised to do. We visited for a bit, but before leaving and I told him who I was related to because I damn well knew he would hear it from someone else, probably the same day, if he didn't already know. He looked straight at me and ask, "Are you like your brothers?" I immediately said, "No sir, I'm not, never have been, and never plan to be." He thanked me for sharing this information but somehow or another, I think he already knew. He told me some months later that two people had heard he had breakfast with me and told him I was Gary Tison's sister. He said, "I told them I already knew, because you had told me yourself upon our first meeting." He assured me, at this point, he had no intentions of doing business with these small-minded individuals in the future, which confirmed what mother had always told me "Be honest, it's always best."

My speech that day at the conference was about ethics, of all things, as it was an important topic for me when dealing with other people's money either by trusting me with their money for investment purposes, purchase of a home, or commercial property. I spent nights on my speech after working, after putting the kids to bed ... it was going to be epic!

I spent the entire day prior washing my car (they weren't even going to see it, but it was important to me), haircut, nails, even shaving my legs, like that was important to anyone but me. Everything had to be perfect when I walked into that conference because this is the type of goal, I'd set for myself and worked so hard to obtain. I always knew in my heart I was more than that ugly, skinny kids from the south side of the tracks and had set numerous goals for myself. This one was above and beyond my wildest dreams.

Before taking my seat, I ran to the lady's room. With the stall door closed, I heard two women enter. Reapply their make-up, one said to the other, "State must be desperate for a speaker, I understand they have Gary Tison's sister speaking today, this should be interesting." I wasn't sure how she knew this but then, I never knew who knew and who didn't, usually not until derogatory comments were made. My heart fell, all pride dropped from my heart, and I literally wanted to flush myself down the toilet. That old song by Frankie Valli came to mind .... "Big Girls Don't Cry." Bullshit! I wanted to cry so badly but I kept myself from doing so, as I didn't have any make-up to fix myself up and felt fairly sure the "ladies" who were talking about me wouldn't lend me theirs had I introduced myself. I waited for them to leave and immediately found a pay phone to call my mom, who was my personal support group throughout this whole escapade and in many other areas. After telling her what transpired in the lady's room, there was a bit of a pause, she then gently said, "You pull yourself up by your own bootstraps, take a deep breath and hit it again. You walk onto that stage with pride and knowing you were the one who was asked to speak, not either of the two women in the lady's room, you remember that."

My mother used the term *bootstraps* a lot with me over the years, and I always thought it a bit entertaining, as my mother probably never had a pair of boots on in her life, especially cowboy boots with pull up straps ... but somehow, I always found it motivating and used it with my own children over the years. Taking a couple minutes for me to refocus, take a few deep breaths, and walk upon that stage to take my seat with the gentleman who was master of ceremonies for this event and others I didn't know. In my thoughts, I kept pulling at absolutely every positive thing I could think of to not burst out in tears and want to run away and hide.

He introduced me as "the speaker for the conference," and I received a warm welcome ... but of course, they didn't know at that time who I was, perhaps only the two ladies from the restroom did, and I didn't know who they were or where they were sitting. I always am smiling; it came easy for me even during trying times and I look back in retrospect and realized I was quite attractive, thin, and fit, so I'm sure that helped with the warm welcome.

After the introduction, I said, "My speech today is on ethics. When folks trust us for often, the biggest investment of their lives, ethics should be first and foremost in our thoughts as Realtors." I did more investments along with my investors than I did the traditional selling of Real Estate, as there was always commission on the table and felt it wasn't right that I did all the work and some Realtor who brought in a buyer/investor walked away with 6-10% of the sale. It was after the first commercial investment that I decided I needed to obtain a real estate license so I could handle the sale and collect half, if not all, of the commission.

After telling them I was the mother of three beautiful children, and wife of Frank (Boomer) who was a college professor, etc. etc. and right at that moment I decided to go for it or run away and hide.... that "fight or flight attitude" I had adapted as a young girl kicked in, and I went for it! I knew for sure there were at least two women in this audience that knew who I was, and I decided to tell them all ... a real game changer for my future.

I looked across the audience of 500, smiled a warm, friendly smile and said, "As some of you may know and some don't, I am Gary Tison's sister." The news of the escape and history of my father and brothers was still prevalent on the news, so of course, everyone knew of it. The place got dead quiet; I could hear a guy breathing on the second row. I let that sink in for a moment, and then reminded them that what they do on a normal daily business, which they might consider just shrewd business, for me it would be criminal, if it ever came down to brass tacks due to who I was related to. By keeping this in mind, reminding them to be always vigil and honest with others investment/ money and should be the first consideration in their daily business, not just getting the escrow closed so they could pick up their commission checks.

I spoke for approximately an hour, strictly on ethics, and thanked them all for giving me the opportunity of speaking at their annual convention. To my surprise, I received a standing ovation and applauds, that lasted like what seemed forever. My self-esteem had been reinstated and from that point on I made the decision to never, ever bow down to another human due to being a Tison. Instead, I would stand tall and be proud of what I had accomplished on my own. That day changed my life forever.

I immediately found another pay phone to call my mother and tell her how well it went and that I had been honest. She was so proud and said she wanted us to come to dinner at her house and celebrate; she even made a little cake. She was my biggest cheerleader, who always knew my heart ... My mother.

***

A few months after, Frank and I were going to the annual Vaquero's Foundation Fundraiser held by Central Arizona College. It was always the best event of the season in our area, and we both looked forward to it each year. It was a full day of good food, lots of booze, good, longtime friends and loads of laughter. It was one of the fundraisers that you hoped your ticket *Did Not Win* as the winner at the end each year received a substantial prize, which one year was a $10,000 bond, and we won it along with a friend. Part of the fun of this event would be to attempt to buy one or more of the remaining tickets if yours had already been drawn ... getting yourself back to having the final ticket. That particular year, it got down to our ticket and a friend. He knew we wouldn't sell ours so suggested he and Frank go up and take the prize together, which they did.

Frank was dedicated to CAC and loved being a professor. He once told me with his degrees, experience, and knowledge, he could make ten times the money he did in the industry, but that he loved teaching. I assured him he should do what he loved, and I'd run our different businesses and make the money with his help.

As we drove out to The Property Conference Center, just about a quarter mile from the center, we couldn't help but notice all the cop car lights at a local business. That business belonged to my brother, Larry. He had always lived in the Flagstaff area with his wife and children, but when things went sour for him, for whatever reason, he came back to Casa Grande. Looking back, all my brothers did this, though I never quit understood why. Surely, they knew local police would watch him closer than anyone else due to the history of all their criminal activity.

He came to my house one day and told me he had wished he had kept his life free from criminal activity and listen to me as a kid, saying I had made it without breaking the law and he felt he could too if given another chance. Even knowing what I knew about my brothers and that they could lie so easily and persuade someone to do something that they would never consider doing for anyone else ... I lent him several thousand dollars to start what he told me would be a mechanical shop. He was probably one of the best mechanics I had ever known and knew he could make a good living at it, if he just tried. I insisted Frank never knew about the loan and that if he got in trouble again, I wasn't going to be there to help. Everyone deserves a second chance, and I gave him one ... although this was probably far more than his second chance, but he seemed so sincere about wanting to live a normal, crime-free life.

As Frank I slowly drove by on our way to the Vaqueros Foundation fundraiser, he looked at me and said, "Do you want to stop?" I honestly thought he was running a mechanical shop but knew at that moment that he was probably running a chop shop, not a mechanical repair shop. I also knew I never would see my money from the loan and that once again I'd been sucked in by a family member and that public embarrassment was sure to follow.

I took Frank's hand, looked him in the eyes, and said, "I'm sorry. As you know, we're gonna pay for this publicly. Do you want to still attend the fundraiser?" He assured me he did as we'd done nothing wrong and that nobody would even know it was one of my brothers.

Of course, everyone else in attendance had seen what we saw, but fortunately for me that day, they didn't know it was one of my brothers until the 6:00 o'clock news and the next day's newspaper, then my phone started ringing continuously until I unplugged it for peace of mind. Those calling knew what I knew, which was what the news was reporting. Apparently thinking they thought I'd give them some insight and I knew nothing except I wasn't going to be paid back the money Larry borrowed, having to explain it to Frank, public shame once again for their criminal activity and my own disgust for trusting one of them again.

It surely wasn't the first time I had been embarrassed by a family member and probably wouldn't be the last, as they chose a life of crime and would most likely continue in the path until they were locked up for forever or dead, which they did.

Final Chapter

It was a long, hard road from the south side of the tracks to the beautiful home I now live in, and the financial security I've been blessed with, but I always knew I would make it. A good, clean life paid off for me and my children and my late husband Frank "Boomer" Williams, whom I still miss terribly.

My family and I paid a horrendous price for the things our father and brothers did. Even now, forty plus years after Gary's escape, it still surfaces periodically, and we never know who knows and who doesn't know who we are related too. Although all my long-time friends and locals know and have accepted me on face value as I've proven myself over and over in this community to be a solid, well-adjusted person who contributes to society. Over the years, I've had many folks ask me about different things and was always hesitant to go into any detail about the family's dysfunction I had grown up in and how I attempted to overcome it in my life. This was one of the deciding factors in writing this book even after all this time. I have friends from grade school that I still socialize with, and only now will they finally learn what it was like for me growing up with career criminals.

Shortly after the escape, I met and married Frank. I jokingly said for years that "He loved the kids and married me so he could father them and be a part of their lives; I was just part of the deal." He never had any children of his own. We had a great life together till his death in 2011 and there was never any doubt that these were his children, and he, their father. I never heard the word *stepfather* or *stepchildren* in our home by their own choice. Being common knowledge with those who knew us that where one of us was the other wasn't too far away.

He was an active part of the Coolidge's Sheriff's Posse for many years and rode horses through the desert with other posse members when law enforcement was looking for Gary after he escaped the roadblock south of town. He learned I was in no way like any of them, had set myself apart from them, had high morals and good work ethics and decided he wanted to spend the rest of his life with me.

Just before he slipped into a coma, I sat at his feet while he was in his recliner, and he said to me "You and the kids have been everything to me; marrying you was the best decision I ever made, and the worst part of death is leaving you and the kids." I assured him he was the strongest man I'd ever met, and he could continue to fight this cancer, however he took my hands and said, "Lynda I've been fighting this for three and a half years. I'm tired. Please forgive me for leaving you but we have great kids and friends, and you have a strong support system, you will be fine." Within an hour, he went into a coma, and I kept my promise to him earlier about staying at the ranch till the end.

The double doors leading into our bedroom remained open with soft lighting. I brought the doctor to him rather than take him to a hospital, honoring my word to keep him home. Our kids, grandkids and friends were there for a week till his final breath. The house was full of loving, caring people, and somehow, I knew he felt this. Often there would be kids and grandkids laying or sitting on the bed talking to him and laughing about good memories. He never moved or flinched, but I somehow knew he was aware they were there. He loved having a big extended family even though he would often joke about them coming around as adults, drinking all his beer, eating all the food, thrashing the house, and leaving and he loved every moment of it, especially the time of year when we made loads of tamales for our annual Christmas hayride.

On his last night, I lay next to him till early hours of the morning and told him I understood that he had to leave and how tired he was from fighting this cancer. I reminisced about the years of our flying an airplane and then onto boating with a 40' ocean cruiser, which we both learned together and often, the hard way. I assure him I did have strong support to move forward and that we would always keep his memory alive, which we have. To this day, whenever we are together, there are always funny Boomer stories told.

During the late night when I was reminiscing with him about our life together, I told many funny stories that I prayed his subconscious would pick up and to reconfirm that we had a great life together. More laughter than tears and in my opinion, that is a good marriage. One of the many stories I told him during that night was of our trip to Canada in 1993 for training he required for the college. We traveled frequently but always fly to wherever and rented a car, however this time, he insisted we drive, attend the Calgary Stampede, and enjoy the beauty of this country which we surely did. We then traveled onto Edmonton, spending a week while he was in training, then west through the Canadian Rockies which I believe is as close to heaven as one can get on earth. We continued onto a ferry to the Island of Victoria where we stayed in the Impress Hotel. It had been built in the 1800's at a cost of $300,000. and had just had a $300 M make over the year we arrived. What a fabulous place! I decided to enjoy high tea and he thought he would pass on that, being the cowboy type, so he choose to go to a bar and drink a Beer. However, it backfired on him, as no service in a bar during high tea.

As we traveled again by ferry back into the U.S., we drove through the Red Woods on the California coastline. I had told him the stories about growing up and it seemed every other kid in school brought a picture to school at the beginning of the school year of their family driving their car thru one of those huge trees. Growing up, we were shipped to California to pick fruit in the summer and back to Arizona to chop cotton in the fall. Never having experienced such a vacation, I insisted I drive my car through one of those trees. I remembered him laughing at me and telling me I probably would tear off the side mirrors of my beautiful new Lincoln, but it didn't matter to me ..... I was finally going to drive through one of those trees like pictures I'd seen in grade school of the rich kids who had visited there on their summer vacations. He grabbed the camera and went to the other side of the tree to capture this big moment for me. Yes!! I did finally get to drive through and put the picture on the refrigerator when returning home. I didn't tear the mirrors off, but I did scratch them up pretty good. He just laughed and said "OK my sweet Lynda, you finally got to do it". These were the type stories I told him while he just lay there slipping deeper into death. He died right at daybreak, which was his favorite time of day. He turned to face me just before he took his last breath, and I knew it had taken all the strength he had left to do so. It was his way of saying goodbye to me.

To this day, I still don't know how so many learned of his death so quickly. Before the funeral car even came to take him, folks were showing up and just going into our shop nearby; they didn't come into the house, as they knew we were waiting for the funeral car to take him, but they just wanted us to know they were there and close. We had numerous parties in our shop over the years, so most everyone we knew was familiar with the bar and kitchen area. The bar was full, someone built a fire in the pot-bellied stove, and coffee and sandwiches were being prepared in the kitchen. I walked out our back door at one point just to catch my breath, only to see a good friend Ronnie, drive his truck up to the flagpole, get out and do a slow salute to the American flag we flew. That touched my heart, and I realized how blessed we have always been with dear friends and still are.

When I first met Frank, he owned a small ranch about twelve miles east of Casa Grande and had horses and cattle. The first time we drove down the three-quarters of a mile dirt road to enter the ranch, there was a sign that read "Dead End." He stopped by the sign and told me he loved me and wanted to build a life with the kids and me on this ranch. He said, "If you continue down this road with me right now, there is no turning back ... it's forever." I was frightened, as I had been married at a young age, and it didn't turn out so well; my first husband was an abuser and womanizer just like my father, and I just wasn't sure I wanted to do that again. I shared my fears and feelings with Frank, and he gave me his word, while placing his hand over his heart, that he would never do either, and he didn't.

I lived in Casa Grande with my children when we met, and Frank was living on the ranch in a travel trailer. He explained since he worked all the time, that was sufficient for him, but that he looked forward to building our home and living there with me and the kids.

Shortly after we married, I realized one of the neighbors near the ranch had a problem with "a Tison" living there. My thoughts were *what the hell, here we go again."* This lady had a pretty rough reputation with everyone who knew her for sleeping around both before and after her marriage and was probably the most hated woman I had ever encountered in the entire area. She was arrogant and she felt I was far beneath her due to my family. She made my life a living hell for the first couple of years I lived there. I had dealt with this type of behavior my entire life and felt I no longer was going to tolerate it. Finally, I told Frank to deal with this with her husband or I would move back into town. He did, and she rarely ever came around after that, although I would see her at social gatherings, always keeping my distance from such a negative, self-absorbed person. The family who lived at the Pecan Orchard right at the turn off to my ranch, were warm, friendly, and welcoming from the beginning, and we became good, lasting friends to this day. Had it not been for this beautiful family, so full of love and acceptance, I doubt I would have made it living out there on the ranch. They warned me about the other neighbor and insisted I pay her no attention as no one else did in the neighborhood.

However, one day when she knew Frank wouldn't be there, she came and decided to take my horse Prissy back to her farm, as she insisted, I didn't know enough about horses to have such a good one. Frank had given me this beautiful Quarter Horse as a wedding present, had raised her from a colt. She also told me she instructed her boys to not ever, ever come here, as I was a bad person due to my family and they could be in danger. Holy crap, I lost it, and it did not turn out well for her. I had taken abuse for my father and brothers my entire life and had decided it would no longer continue, at least not in my new home on the ranch. I took the reins out of her hand and reminded her I was a "Tison" and she didn't want to know how we handled anger. I decided to use this on my behalf for one of the few times in my life, and she couldn't get out of there fast enough. I still chuckle when I think of this encounter with such a horrible excuse for a human being.

We worked on building our home; every weekend and holidays was spent out there laying and grouting out blocks that were already strong with rebar. Frank told me he didn't know how to build houses, but he knew how to build bridges, so we built the house like a bridge, often standing side by side, as we nailed up the framing. Installed insulation, etc. We encountered numerous comments, usually done in jest, as we continued about just how much strong structure was in the house. When it came in insulation time, that got even more detailed, as he insulated more than once saying he had heard of older folks not being able to afford utilities in their homes on a fixed income after retirement, and he swore that wouldn't happen to us.

He chuckled one day while sitting on the edge of the fireplace drinking a beer that he hoped he lived long enough to see some SOB try to tear the place down, as it was built strong. Unfortunately, he didn't have that opportunity, but I did. He died in 2011 and a few years ago I got into a lengthy battle with a major power company out of Florida that purchased all the property surrounding my ranch. According to my second son, who is an Engineer with experience in the solar field, and worked as my consultant during the legal battle, it was his determination based on studies/reports that the solar panels surrounding my ranch could cause the temperatures to rise as high as 137 degrees during the summer months, making it impossible for my horses or myself to remain there. The solar panels would start within ten feet of my pool and one of my pastures. The legal battle was expensive, lengthy, and emotionally draining for me, as I was also already having health issues and was hospitalized many times during this process. I was so incredibly grateful for my son and our friend, Gilbert, a legal expert having just retired from the bench, who handled the legal issues and ultimately got me a nice settlement.

After the settlement, the three of us had a good laugh about how we were the only ones we knew who would take on a $17 billion company ... and win.

After leaving the ranch and moving to town, a neighbor called to tell me they were tearing down the house. I gave it some thought before heading out there, not sure if it was a good idea or not emotionally but decided to go. I felt lightheaded and physically sick, as I saw more than half of the house already torn down, like a hurricane had hit it. When I got myself together and got out of my truck, a guy walked up, and we introduced ourselves; he was the general demolition contractor. He made the comment about the house being difficult for him to tear down, as it was so beautiful; he had even offered to purchase it from the power company, but due to reports the power company knew nobody could live there with the solar power structures being built, so denied his offer.

As we were talking, an older man got off a heavy piece of equipment, walked up to me, wiped his hands off on his jeans, shook my hand, and said, "Lady I've been tearing down structures for fifty years, but I have never, ever seen anything like this. I can usually take out a swimming pool in four hours, but I've been on yours for two days. Where in the hell did you and your late husband acquire so much rebar?"

I chuckled, shook his hand, and said, "You have just made my husband's day as I know he just heard you even though he has been gone for a while. He wanted to live long enough to watch some SOB try to tear it down as it was his desire to build it strong, and apparently he did ... thank you."

My heart was so heavy from all the memories, both good and bad of living and running a ranch, but I was glad I had gone out there to see it for myself. As I got about halfway to the main highway, I started crying and couldn't stop. Sitting there in my truck, I'd never felt so alone ... my husband gone, children grown, a power company basically moving me out against my wishes and moving into town which I didn't want to do. We won the legal battle, and I was well paid, however with the transient family lifestyle I had grown up in, the ranch was the longest I'd ever lived in one place, and the W6 Ranch held all my hopes and dreams with my family with Frank's ashes being scatter there after his death. I handled it though like the educated, professional I am ... I went to the bar and got drunk.

Frank struggled with cancer of the throat in the early 1980s. We did radiation in a Tucson facility, and he recovered. Unfortunately, it reoccurred years later and had a devastating effect for himself and our entire family. While he was in surgery the first time around with the cancer, one of my brothers and another family member entered my home by picking a lock and stole two freezers full of beef from a steer we had recently butchered, some bonds, jewelry, and mattress cash from the sale of some cattle. One of the irrigators described the two, and I knew exactly who it was. I called my brother Joe and told him that this was a low, even for him, to come into my home and rob us while my husband was fighting for his life in surgery. He just laughed and said, "Aw hell, you got insurance, don't you?" After that, I had a high-tech security system installed, and told him not to come around again ever, ever. I was too embarrassed to make a police or insurance report, as I didn't want to have to explain my dysfunctional family and that it was two of them who had robbed me. I knew it would be in the newspapers, and I felt it best to eat the loss due to embarrassment.

The second time around with the cancer, Frank had numerous major surgeries to remove cancer and was sent home the morning of Good Friday and was considered critical. Because of Good Friday, I was unable to reach his surgeon but learned on Monday that he was released by mistake. Holy cow – the hospital had medical equipment delivered that I didn't even know how to turn on, much less operate, and Frank's life depended on it. In a panic, I called a friend of mine who was a nurse, ask her to help me and she dropped what she was doing, which I learned later, was coloring Easter eggs with her grandchildren. She came to the ranch immediately. I've been so very blessed with good friends over the years. She explained in no uncertain terms that she could not touch him or the equipment due to liability issues, but that she would instruct and train me, which she did. I am forever grateful to her.

He had a stoma, which is difficult to clean and clear, and necessary for him to breath, and I had learned about this while being in the hospital with him so much. However, the equipment was an entirely different scenario. Thank God for my friend!

He required 24/7 care and with a feeding tube, I had to feed him every four hours like a newborn through his tube for the first fourteen months. My daughter DeAnna became such an asset to me, as she came to the ranch and helped with him whenever she wasn't working. She ultimately took a sabbatical from work and was able to be there on a regular basis, and I can't tell you what a relief that was to me, to say I was overwhelmed was an understatement and still running my water treatment equipment company. I felt terrible for her, though, as she lost all her seniority, but I was so thankful for the help. As I look back in retrospect, I have absolutely no idea how I did this for three and a half years. During that time frame, I took two days while Frank was being cared for by a nurse. I went to a hotel and slept for fourteen hours, got food, showered, and slept for another fourteen hours. I worried about his possible passing while I was gone so decided I needed to be there with him, although the rest helped tremendously, and I felt I was ready to take it all on again. He looked so happy, like a child, when I returned and I vowed to never leave his side again, which I didn't.

I explained to Frank that he was my priority, however, I still had a business and was being pulled in several directions at once. Lalo who was my right arm for the business, slowly took over, and is still running it today. I was so grateful to him as after the first couple of years, customers were no longer asking for me but rather Lalo. I knew then he had become the face of my company and should own it rather than work for it, which I made happen.

Along with my family and friends, I also had Garrett for support and assistance. Garrett came into our life's years earlier through the college, became like a son and after Frank became sick, he kept my farm equipment and trucks serviced, always seem to be there when I needed him, and I'm grateful to both young men who are still a big part of my life and family and helped salvaged me in my time of need.

Garrett sent me the below note after our 2020 family Thanksgiving dinner, and it touched my heart to the depths:

Last night you said we are living proof that we don't have to be blood to be family. On our way home last night a thought occurred to me. We're living proof that God works in the most mysterious ways. He is telling us that we are all part of His family. It doesn't matter who are real parents are, what color we are, our age, our thought differences and so on. We didn't just all happen to meet each other. It's been the Lord's plan all along.

I didn't need another family, but God put me in yours for a reason. Boomer offered me a job before he even knew me. I wasn't some broke student he felt sorry for, and he didn't hire me because I wore my hat right. God put me in Boomer's class for a reason. I was chosen to take over for Boomer at the college, and the college is my livelihood. You and Boomer didn't meet on accident or by chance. Your kids needed a dad, and God gave them one.

Thanks for always being there for Britt and I and the kids. You have a beautiful family, and we are blessed to be part of it. Your faith in God helps me keep my faith in Him. He's worked through your life to get to mine. It's amazing to me to look back and see His work. He's let us make our own choices and we've failed at times, but we've always had each other to lean on. You never judged me; you were there when I needed encouragement. God gave me you. I'm so grateful because I have been truly blessed with a family I got to raise and care for. You and Boomer are a huge part of that.

Garrett

God has blessed me in abundance with good people who I often refer to as "My Guardian Angels."

Time has passed and "Life" goes on but always with precious memories of my life with Frank and the kids growing up on the ranch. As for this "Tison" thing, it still surfaces from time to time, however I'm stronger now and feel I can handle almost anything that comes my way.

I'm grateful for the Faith in God that mother instilled in me, and I continue to live a Christian life with God at the core of everything.

Never be a prisoner of your past ....
It was meant to be a lesson, not a life sentence

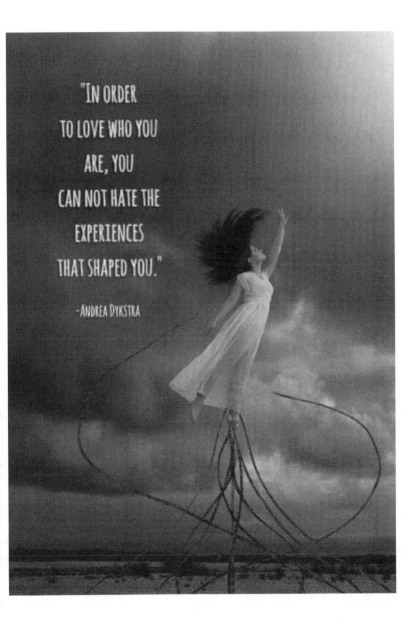

"IN ORDER
TO LOVE WHO YOU
ARE, YOU
CAN NOT HATE THE
EXPERIENCES
THAT SHAPED YOU."

-ANDREA DYKSTRA

ABOUT THE AUTHOR

I am retired after many years of working with abused children/youth, as well as owning and operating other businesses, including a ranch. Widowed in 2011 by the love of my life ... Frank (Boomer) Williams, I am blessed to be a mother of three adult children, grandmother and great-grandmother. It was not an easy task to get from the south side of the tracks to where I now am. God's plan for me from the beginning was beyond my wildest dreams and imagination.

www.lyndawilliamsauthor.com

Made in the USA
Las Vegas, NV
23 October 2021

32921802R10151